C D

This book is to be returned on or before
the last date stamped below.

1 3 OCT 2011

31434

m

media

MANUAL

The Video Studio

Third Edition

Alan Bermingham,
Michael Talbot-Smith,
Ken Angold-Stephens
and Ed Boyce

Focal Press
An imprint of Butterworth-Heinemann Ltd
Linacre House, Jordan Hill, Oxford OX2 8DP

 A member of the Reed Elsevier plc group

OXFORD LONDON BOSTON
MUNICH NEW DELHI SINGAPORE SYDNEY
TOKYO TORONTO WELLINGTON

First published as *The Small Television Studio*, 1975
Second edition 1990
Third edition 1994

British Library Cataloguing in Publication Data
Bermingham, Alan
  Video Studio. – 3Rev.ed. – (Media Manual
  Series)
  I. Title II. Series
  621.3886

ISBN 0 240 51392 4

Library of Congress Cataloguing in Publication Data
The Video Studio/Alan Bermingham . . . [et al.]. – 3rd ed.
  p.   cm. – (Media manuals)
  Includes bibliographical references.
  ISBN 0 240 51392 4
  1. Television stations.   I. Bermingham, Alan.   II. Series.
  TK6646.V53   94–3408
  621.388'6–dc20   CIP

Printed and bound in Great Britain by
Biddles Ltd, Guildford and King's Lynn

Contents

Introduction

The motives behind deciding to develop into video are diverse. At first the challenge may seem daunting. Yet many companies have made a great success of the venture, often starting from modest beginnings. Others have fallen by the wayside, often because they had not thought through how video was to be used or the scale of commitment in terms of staff and investment. How often has a personnel director been asked to buy 'some equipment' only to find it leads to disappointment when it is discovered that the equipment is inappropriate or that professional results seem elusive or impossible? Most professions require years of training. Even more important in television is flair, imagination, experience and a generous amount of enthusiasm!

The clear lesson from the history of video is that there is no place for the sub-standard product if you expect to be taken seriously. Your audience is too sophisticated, being saturated with professionally made programmes every day of their lives.

With that word of caution, television has, nevertheless, achieved enormous success in a vast range of applications, e.g. education, advertising, in-company training for job skills etc., and has even expanded into local access television with the advent of cable services.

How to start

First assess your precise requirements. For example, discussions and conferences are probably best covered by multi-camera techniques, but for documentary and drama single camera techniques may be more appropriate.

Investment in a studio can be modest or considerable. Fast turnrounds between types of programmes imply a high investment in flexible lighting systems which are less labour intensive but expensive. If professionally equipped, consider the possibility of hiring out your studio when not using it yourself. It could pay for itself. Above all, hire a consultant engineer to make sure you get the right advice. If you need to get out and about, for example, into the factory to see manufacturing processes, your studio could be equipped with lightweight cameras that can be de-rigged for portable use. Another alternative is to mount your control room into a vehicle for complete mobility, with the ability to couple up to your studio when necessary.

A more modest, but no less effective, technique is to use one camera with appropriate peripherals to shoot entirely on location; though this is more time consuming and requires a big investment in post-production.

The following pages should give you an insight into the requirements for a professional installation, whether studio or location based.

Acknowledgements

For permission to publish this book, Ken Angold-Stephens thanks the Managing Director Resources of the BBC, and Ed Boyce thanks the Chief Executive of Meridian Broadcasting. John Symon's contribution to the first edition is gratefully acknowledged.

Studio: Initial Planning

Here are some questions which need to be answered at the initial planning stage.

The studio's function
What is the function of the studio, what types of production are envisaged and, most important, how much money is there available for the project?

The possible size of the viewing audience and of the budget available depend directly on the function of the studio, whether it be university CCTV, educational TV to a widely dispersed audience, industrial training, a 'professional' small TV studio producing inserts to a large TV network, medical teaching, producing television commercials, pop promos, corporate video etc.

The types of production to be mounted affect the studio area (see page 18) and the facilities required.

What turn-round time is required between productions? A quick turn-round requires more staff and/or greater flexibility from the studio facilities to meet changing production requirements.

What post-production facilities will the complex require?

Remote productions
Are all the programmes to be carried out in the studio? If location work is required, e.g. on-the-job training, this could be covered either by a film crew or by using a mobile control room. The mobile control room could also be used for the studio productions on a 'drive-in' basis, i.e. it could be parked adjacent to the studio, and the camera cables, microphone cables etc. would be run from it to the studio.

This may be a solution to the problem of trying to mount studio and location productions on a limited budget.

Constructional considerations
Where should the studio be located? If it is to be part of a school or university, it must be adjacent to the 'consumer', unless the studio is to feed a large number of consumers by radio or cable links. If there is a free choice of location, 'man-made' hazards for sound insulation should be avoided—motorways, railways, airports. Local high-powered radio transmitters can also cause interference problems.

Will the studio be purpose-built or be in a converted existing building? Suitable buildings in the correct location are not easy to find. The main factor to bear in mind is the height required in the studio (see page 18).

Finally—what about future expansion? The philosophy should be optimistic—try to see where possible expansions may take place—extra studio area, new studio, etc.

Typical planning considerations

General

● Intended function of television facilities	Educational, industrial training, broadcast (commercial or other uses), medical teaching etc.
● Types of production	Package programmes, interviews, presentations, demonstrations, commercials etc.
● Frequency of use	Daily use requires more staff and greater investment in equipment flexibility to achieve faster turn-rounds.
● Commercially viable or 'in-house' use only?	If programmes are to be sold or hired (particularly to broadcasters) or if facilities are to be hired out, broadcast or near-broadcast facilities will be required.

Technical resources

● Broadcast or non-broadcast facilities	Dependent on above considerations, with major cost implications.
● Manning arrangements	Local or freelance staff or a combination of both.
● Method of programme realization	Studio or single location camera unit or combination of both.
● Investment costs	Dependent on above factors. Full broadcast equipment is dramatically more expensive than even slightly down-market equivalent.
● Depreciation	Depends on equipment and its usage. Could be as short as 3 years for some equipment, as long as 10 years for others.
● Running costs	Production, crewing and maintenance costs must be added to those above and should include (where appropriate) wardrobe, make-up, artistes' fees, location costs etc.

Studio Facilities

The size of the studio, and the scale and type of production, determine our precise requirements. However, at the upper end of our survey (the studio of 150 m²) there is a need for comprehensive facilities. These can be categorised as technical, production and post-production

Technical: vision facilities (including lighting)
               sound facilities (including talkback and communications)
               recording facilities
Production: scenic design
               graphic design
               costume design
               make-up design

Technical facilities
Technical facilities are usually permanent features within a studio and its associated environs, and do not change on a day-to-day basis.

The upper illustrations opposite show the possible vision and sound sources for a production. The various 'boxes' we see here are examined in detail in later pages.

Production requirements
Production requirements, on the other hand, change from one programme to the next. In order to meet typical production requirements, the various functions shown in the lower illustration are needed.

Post-production requirements
Most studio complexes require post-production facilities ranging from simple videotape editing using two machines to multi-machine editing facilities complete with digital effects and digital graphics.

There is also a need to consider a sound dubbing suite for post-production work on both location and studio-produced programmes.

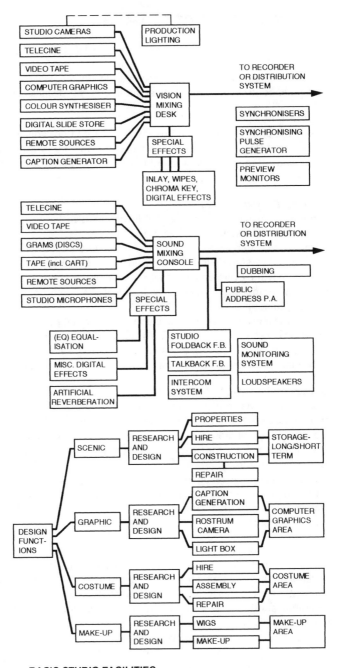

BASIC STUDIO FACILITIES

15

Layout of Control Areas

The three main control areas associated with a TV studio are:
● Production control: director and his immediate production staff.
● Vision control area: lighting director and video engineers/operators.
● Sound control area: sound mixer audio control specialist and his staff.

Location near the studio
Ideally the control area should be on the ground floor adjacent to the studio. There should be quick and easy access into the studio from all the control areas, and of course artistes should not have to go through control areas to gain access to the studio.

Observation windows
Large double-glazed windows should be included between all control areas to enable good visual communication.

The current trend is not to include observation windows between control areas and the studio floor. Their value is debatable in that they are often obscured by the cyclorama or the scenery. However, if included they should:
● Be large and double-glazed with at least 600 mm (2 ft) gap to maintain sound insulation.
● Include a venetian blind to exclude studio lighting spilling onto monitors.
● Ideally, be colour corrected with a blue daylight correction filter on windows between the vision control areas and studios. This enables direct comparison to be made between colour picture monitors and the studio scene.

Communal control area
Sharing the same control room has the advantage of the economy of monitors and loudspeakers and easy communications between staff. Usually, however, the sound control area is made into an acoustically isolated area to minimise the disturbance to the rest of the production team from high levels of loudspeaker volume.

Multi-skilling has resulted in fewer staff being required, often, for example, a director may also vision mix or an engineer may control the video-tape replays, shot selection (remote cameras) and also look after lighting and vision control operations.

Separate control areas
The third basic arrangement is usually adopted in larger studios. It has the advantage that it completely isolates the functions, so that the staff can concentrate more easily on their particular tasks. However, a comprehensive communication system and many more monitors and loudspeakers are required in this layout.

Finally, equipment which generates excessive noise and heat should be excluded, e.g. telecine and videotape machines should have a separate area, as should the lighting dimmers controlling the studio lamps.

Basic combined control room with multi skilling manning

1. Sound supervisor
2. Vision supervisor
3. Director
4. Production assistant
5. Technical manager
6. Tape and grams operator
7. Vision mixer
8. Lighting director
9. Vision control operator
10. Caption control operator

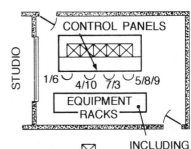

Control room complex using a separate sound control room

An alternative would be to position the sound area in a room behind the production team, on a raised floor to enable the sound staff to see the production staff/monitors through a large observation window. They would however still need at least two picture monitors, transmission and switchable.

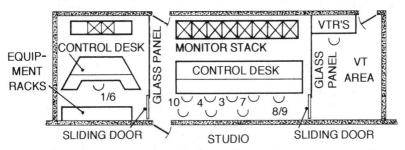

Multi-control room complex using separate control rooms

Remember to cater for staff requiring access to control rooms during operations, i.e., producers, programme editors, scenic designers, make-up designs etc.

This can simply be by the provision of additional high chairs.

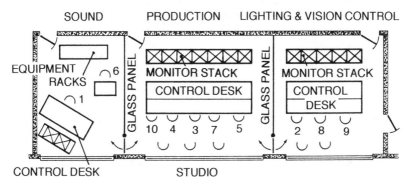

17

Studio Construction

The studio has to provide an environment that allows all operations to be carried out in reasonable comfort and absolute safety. Factors to be considered when designing a studio or when looking for a suitable building to convert into a studio are as follows.

Area, shape and height
The area required depends on the use for which the studio is intended. The relative sizes of studios and their uses are shown opposite.

The proportions of the studio (width: length) are important for the larger studio if the maximum utilisation of the available area is to be achieved and cameras/booms are to cover the area easily. It should be within the range of 1:1.1 to 1:1.5; preferably close to 1:1.3. A ratio of 1:1 is undesirable because it can give rise to unsatisfactory acoustics.

The structural height required is often a neglected factor, particularly when existing buildings are converted into small TV studios. The minimum height required can be determined by considering:
- Height of the cyclorama cloth or scenery needed to avoid shooting-off.
- Suspension system required for the lighting equipment.
- Space occupied by ventilation systems (trunking, outlets).

Floor, walls and ceiling
Except for situations in which the camera is absolutely static, the studio floor should be horizontal, level and firm to prevent vibration. A tolerance of 1.6 mm displacement in 3 m should be satisfactory for all but fast-moving camera dollies. A solid floor base is essential. It should be quiet to walk on and firm so that when cameras are moved on it there are no extraneous creaks.

The final surface of the floor should be non-slip, of matt finish, durable, and capable of withstanding continual painting with water-paint followed by washing. Cameras cannot move smoothly over uneven floors, so many surfaces are simulated. Carpets often have to be painted on the floor, as do cobblestones, parquet floors, tiles etc. The unpainted colour of the floor is important too, especially for colour TV. It should be a light neutral (grey) colour so that light reflected from it does not throw a colour cast on the performers' faces.

The studio walls should be as thick as possible to provide good sound insulation, and should be acoustically treated to control reverberation time and sound quality in the studio. Ideally the only windows should be special windows into control rooms.

The ceiling should be strong and thick to provide good sound insulation and to support the lighting and scenic suspension system. For new installations it is desirable to build the studio itself independently from its foundations to the roof, and so prevent structure-borne noises from reaching the studio (see page 24).

18

Typical production requirements

Area	Studio function	Number of cameras
10–15 m²	Presentation news ('talking head' to camera)	1
30 m²	Static 2-way interviews, simple documentary presentations	2
60 m²	Multiple interviews, simple light entertainment, documentary, educational	2/3
150 m²	Interviews, quizzes, simple light entertainment, documentary, educational, small-scale drama	2/3

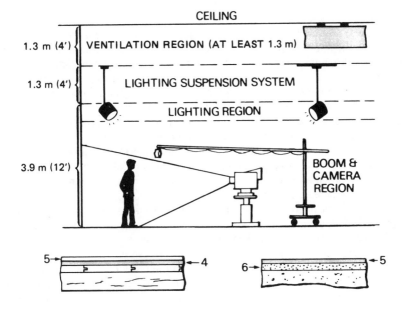

Typical space allocation
A studio should have sufficient height to accommodate various installation services, such as ventilation, lighting suspension. Each tends to use a defined region of the studio space.

Studio flooring
An existing wooden floor may be stiffened by using large sheets of 25 mm (1 in) plywood (4).
The plywood should be screwed every 50 mm (2 in) to the existing floorboards.
In this well-constructed floor, heavy duty linoleum (5) has been laid on carefully levelled asphalt (6) on a concrete foundation.

19

Studio General Services

In addition to the sound, vision, and lighting facilities equipment, the studio needs to have various features to facilitate efficient production.

Access
Ideally the studio should be at ground level, to allow easy access for scenery, props and technical equipment, which may range from grand pianos and motor vehicles to animals of various sizes. The main access should have no ramp or steps, i.e. smooth access.

Studio doors should be large, thick and heavy to provide easy access and to prevent loss of sound insulation. Smaller lightweight sound-trap doors are usually provided, in addition to the larger heavy doors, for ease of use by actors and studio staff (see page 23).

Power and lighting
The power requirements of production lighting in the studio are covered on page 91. In addition, the studio needs standard mains supplies to power studio equipment such as monitors, microphone amplifiers and any electrical equipment used in a particular production. A 13 amp ring-main supply is needed with outlets spaced around the studio walls (at 4 m intervals, say). If it is anticipated that productions will include higher power equipment for demonstrations (e.g. machinery, cookers) then suitable power outlets (30 amp, or even 3-phase supplies) should be provided.

Cable ducts or runways leading supplies into the studio can inadvertently provide a path for external, structure-borne sounds. A 1–2 cm gap in the cable duct provides a cure, but a flexible earth link must be connected across the gap to ensure earth continuity.

Most studios need a supply of gas, hot and cold water, and a drainage system for such applications as cookery, chemistry experiments etc, and staging effects (pools, water displays, domestic situations).

A compressed air feed to the studio is also very useful.

The TV studio must be effectively lit when the production lighting is not in use, to facilitate such studio activities as erecting scenery, preparing equipment etc. These house lights should be able to be switched, both in the studio and at the lighting console.

An emergency lighting system is also essential, and usually includes illuminated exit signs which automatically change over to battery supplies if there is a mains failure.

Studio markings and floor plans
To assist the accurate positioning of scenery, the studio walls should be marked boldly at regular intervals (half-metre or footage marks are typical). The floor can be marked similarly with very light scoring marks to produce a reference grid. For accurate production planning, scale studio floor-plans (staging plans) are essential (page 171).

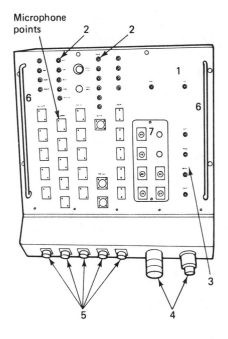

Studio floor and wall markings
The studio walls are clearly marked at ½-metre (or 1 ft) intervals, to facilitate exact positioning of staging and equipment—to conform with the production staging plan. The floor may be lightly scored at ½-metre intervals.

Microphone points

Studio distribution box
Individually identified metal-clad boxes are located at intervals along the studio walls. These contain a series of outlets and supplies for equipment.
1. Distribution box identification.
2. Talkback, switched talkback, audio tie lines.
3. Monitor video feeds, video tie lines.
4. Camera cable plug points.
5. Multi-way microphone connections.
6. 'Tie bar' for cables.
7. Mains sockets (technical mains).

21

Studio Sound Insulation

A television studio should obviously be well insulated from external noise. Good sound insulation is very expensive, however, so there is little point in trying to reduce levels of noise picked up from outside the studio below the internally generated noise level (e.g. camera fan motors, ventilation, etc.). A realistic studio background noise, from noise entirely originating outside the studio, is probably in the region of 30 dBA (roughly 30 dB above the average ear's hearing threshold, assuming appropriate frequency correction).

External noise
There are two types of externally-generated noise entering a studio. First, structure-borne sound is vibration conveyed through the fabric of the building, along water-pipes, etc. Such acoustic interference is usually very costly to cure. Good initial design of the building is often the only sure way to ensure satisfactory insulation. Where structure-borne sound is unacceptable, the only solution may be to stop the noise at source, by switching it off during recording or transmission (e.g. waterpumps). It may be possible, in some cases, to have machinery mounted on resilient supports so that less vibration is transmitted to the building structure.

The second type of noise is airborne and can often be reduced significantly by providing all studio doors with magnetic seals at their edges.

Any windows in the studio walls should be double- or even triple-glazed at wider spacings than are normally used for thermal insulation—e.g. 150 cm (6 in) minimum. If this cannot be done, heavy shutters with good seals at their edges should be fitted. It is worth noting that, as a general rule, the more massive a partition, the better the insulation it provides against airborne noise, although some specially constructed lightweight multiple-skin structures can be effective.

Sound leakage
Sound can leak through very small apertures—hence the need for seals on doors and shutters—and if a studio suffers from airborne noise problems it is worthwhile examining it carefully for such leaks. In particular, entry points for cable ducts, water pipes, etc. may be found to be ineffectively sealed.

Noise from ventilation
Studio ventilation systems can be a source of noise and, unless well designed, often have to be switched off during transmission. In general, a good ventilation system must have large cross-section trunking so that the air is moved relatively slowly. Bends in the trunking are of large radius to reduce turbulence, and the inside walls of the trunking may be lined with sound-absorbent material.

Sound insulation—structural mass

A high proportion of the external noise is airborne. Sound insulation improves as the mass of partitions (walls, floors, ceilings) is increased. Thin, flimsy structures have poor sound insulation.

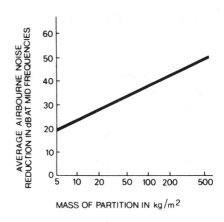

MASS OF PARTITION IN kg/m^2

Sound locks

To prevent external noises being heard when people enter the studio/control rooms, etc., small sound-absorbent cubicles are introduced, known as sound locks. Ideally, ordinary doors should never have direct access into the studio.

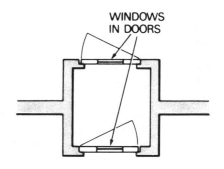

WINDOWS IN DOORS

Door seals

Doors should close as tightly as possible to prevent sound leakage. In addition to closing mechanisms (doors' closers, securing levers, etc.) magnetic door seals set in plastic excluder strips help to ensure firm sealing. 1. Magnetic strip. 2. Mild steel strip.

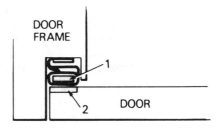

DOOR FRAME

DOOR

Studio Acoustics

Acoustic resonances ('standing waves') can occur as the sound reverberates to and fro between parallel non-absorbent surfaces. The character of the sound picked up by a microphone depends on where it is placed in relation to the intensity pattern of these standing waves.

Acoustical treatment

Acoustic resonances can be avoided by sound *diffusion*. This is usually achieved by introducing deliberate irregularities in the surfaces involved, so that sound waves are scattered when they are reflected.

Standing waves are not normally a serious problem in well-designed television studios, because sound absorbers on the walls reduce the reflected wave energy. Also the presence of technical equipment and scenery provides adequate scattering. However, it can happen that a set contains hard parallel surfaces, so that sound pick-up within it is poor. The best solution here is to alter the set. Opposite walls may be placed non-parallel and made of less acoustically reflecting material—e.g. canvas instead of, say, glass fibre or plywood.

Reverberation time

Reverberation time (RT) is the time taken for a sound in a studio to decay (fade away) through 60 dB. Roughly speaking, this means the time it takes a fairly loud sound to die away to inaudibility. RT is found, approximately, from the Sabine formula (see opposite).

Total sound absorption is the sum of the absorption at all surfaces and is calculated from the area of the surface in square metres, multiplied by the percentage sound absorption for the surface material used.

Reverberation time affects the final quality of the sound considerably. If it is too short, speech tends to sound 'dry' (dead, unreverberant) and orchestral music lacks 'warmth' and 'blend'. Too long a reverberation time, however, makes speech distant and 'echoey'.

Required reverberation times

We normally aim to make a television studio's reverberation time quite short, because reverberation can always be added artificially to the sound output, but can never be taken away.

It is difficult to make a studio of any appreciable size with an extremely short RT, because the floor is inevitably hard and hence non-absorbent to sound, but it is practicable to make a *small* television studio with an RT of 0.3 to 0.5 seconds. This should be acceptable for almost all speech requirements and would also be quite adequate for pop music, where acoustically 'dry' conditions are needed to achieve sufficient separation between the individually balanced sources.

Some typical reverberation times (at mid frequencies)

Open air	nearly zero
Average sitting room	0.5 second
Radio talks studio	0.4 second
Theatre	1.0 second
Large TV studios	0.7 to 1.1 second
Concert halls	1.5 to 2.2 seconds
Large Gothic cathedral	up to 10 or 12 seconds (at low frequencies)

Percentage sound absorption at different frequencies

	60 Hz	1000 Hz	8000 Hz
Rough concrete	1	6	12
Heavy fabrics (draped)	5	80	60
Wood	5	10	15
Plain brick wall	2	4	10
Breeze blocks (unplastered)	13	65	51
Smooth plaster (painted)	1	2	2
Plaster on wood lath	7	13	13
Building board (distempered)	4	19	22
Building board with 25 mm air space	15	20	30
Glass (6 mm) plate	3	3	3

A person seated is equivalent to roughly 0.5 m² of perfect (100%) absorber.

The Sabine formula

$$RT = \frac{0.16 \times \text{volume in m}^3}{\text{Total sound absorption in Sabine units}}$$

1 Sabine unit = 1 m² of 100% absorber. If a = absorption coeffient and s = area (m²), then

$$\text{Total sound absorption} = a_1 s_1 + a_2 s_2 + \ldots \text{ etc.}$$

Studio Ventilation

All ventilation and air-conditioning systems must be considered at the early design stages of the studio complex. Not only the studio itself, but the control rooms, make-up and costume areas, tape and film storage area and technical equipment racks, all have their particular air-control requirements. The studio production lighting generates about 1 kilowatt of heat for every kilowatt of power consumed. This causes a heat build-up which is not only tiring for performers and studio staff alike, but reduces their efficiency considerably.

Preventing heat build-up
Heat build-up in the studio can be reduced to some extent by using:
● Sensitive cameras, and hence lower wattage lamps for the lower light levels needed.
● A lighting console to switch off lamps when they are not in use. A good practice is to start rehearsals with the dimmers set at half their maximum light output (often 7 on the fader), and so produce less heat.
● A high studio ceiling so that the hot air is suspended well above the studio floor.
● A well-planned ventilation and air-conditioning system.
   The function of the ventilation system is to remove the hot air and replace it with cool dry air. The exact requirements are determined by the size of the studio and its commitments, i.e. continuous or intermittent use, small sets or large sets, etc.

General problems
Problems associated with the general system are:
● The scenery will probably not be in identical positions for each production and may sometimes obstruct low-level fresh-air intakes.
● The ventilation system should be capable of changing the studio air several times an hour, i.e. large volumes of air have to be moved. To reduce the noise of the air flow the ventilation ducts should be of large cross sectional area so that the rate of flow of air can be slow (see page 22). One way of overcoming the noise problem cheaply is to use a very fast (but noisy) extraction system intermittently, e.g. during initial rehearsals, recording breaks, etc. Such a system should be fitted with suitable shutters to retain good sound insulation when it is not in use.

Auxiliary requirements
The studio's associated technical and production areas also require air conditioning; otherwise they will become hot and stuffy.
   Technical equipment, especially racks of thyristor dimmers, should have forced ventilation to ensure its stability and reliability.
   The power requirements of the ventilation system should be taken into account at the initial planning stage.

Basic studio ventilation system
If the ventilation system is to be used continuously, it should be capable of handling two-thirds of the maximum lighting power in the form of heat. Use could be made of the extracted hot air for heating the studio complex. With filter (1), cooler (2) and heater (3).

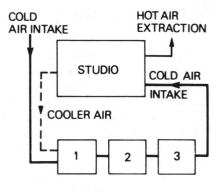

Ventilation trunks
Method of introducing cold air over the top of the scenery by means of large diameter trunks (5).

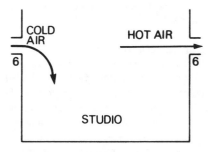

Ventilation shelves
Simple method for introducing cold air and extraction of the hot air by means of two ventilation shelves (6) which extend along the length of the studio.

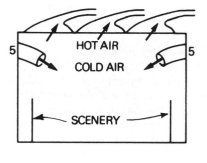

Intermittent usage
Ventilation system for intermittent use (not during transmission or recording). Heavy duty extraction fans (7). Shuttered air vents (8).

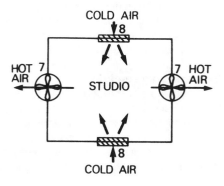

27

Studio Scenery

The type and extent of scenery (staging) required depends on the scale and forms of production envisaged, and on available budgets. There are, however, several basic staging considerations that affect studio design. If the scenery is not sufficiently high, cameras are liable to shoot over it and reveal the studio beyond. To avoid this, the cameras' shots would have to be restricted. For a 150 m² studio, scenery 3 m (10 ft) high should be adequate for most situations. With smaller studios and fairly static situations, less height should suffice, e.g. 2.4 m (8 ft).

For studios on limited budgets, a carefully chosen assortment of stock items can provide useful economies. The paint, like all staging materials, must be fireproof and the range of colours used should be selected to provide good tonal variety.

Classifying colour
The Munsell system of colour classification can prove useful in determining the colour of paint to use to obtain adequate contrast on the monochrome picture. Colours with the same *luminance value* (brightness) on the Munsell colour charts appear approximately the same shade of grey in a monochrome picture provided the camera's colour response is similar to that of the eye. Colours that have the same luminance value as the face (about 6 on the Munsell scale) should be avoided, especially in situations where the scenery and the artiste are lit with the same luminaire, or faces and backgrounds may merge.

Surface treatment
For small, relatively static set-ups, the scenery may often be reduced to a number of decorated sheets or flats which can be clipped to a rail. These can be changed easily and so avoid over-familiarity.

Hard-faced curved scenery should be used with caution—it can cause acoustical problems for sound pick-up.

Floors, when seen in shot, can be specially treated with washable paints. In colour studios care must be taken in choosing a fairly neutral finish, unless a special effect is required. Light reflected from a coloured floor can cause colour casts on the artistes. Where floors are to be painted with designs simulating parquet floors, tiles, etc. special machines incorporating large rollers can be used to provide rapid effective patterns.

Scenic storage and repair
A scenery store with good access to the studio is essential. Otherwise it can become necessary to move spare scenery around the studio just in order to make working floor space available. It should have adequate height to allow the scenery to be stored *vertically*.

A workshop area is normally needed for scenic construction, repair and painting. It should be well ventilated, and acoustically isolated from the studio.

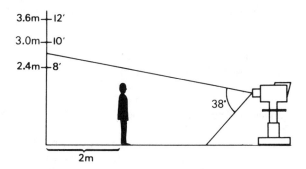

Scenic height
Scenery needs to be about 3 m high if Long Shots are required, otherwise the camera will shoot off.

SURFACE		% REFLECTIVITY	MUNSELL NEUTRAL VALUE	TV SCALE
		100—	—10	
POLISHED SILVER				
WHITE NYLON SHIRTS		90—		
WHITE CARTRIDGE PAPER		80—	—9	
CHROME PLATE				
		70—		
WHITE CLOTH — — — — — — — — — — — —		60 —	—8—	PEAK WHITE
NEWSPAPER		50—		
		40—	—7	LIGHT GREY
EUROPEAN FACES ↕				
LIGHT OAK WOOD		30—	—6	
GREEN LEAVES				
CONCRETE				
DARK SKIN ↕		20—	—5	MED. GREY
BLONDE HAIR		10—	—4	
DARK OAK WOOD				
DARK HAIR			—3	DARK GREY
BLACK PAPER — — — — — — — — — — — —		3—	—2—	BLACK LEVEL
BLACK CLOTH	1%	0—		
BLACK VELVET	0·4%			

Reflectivity scale
Table relating the inherent reflectivities and the Munsell Scale. This illustrates the problem of working with camera tubes which have a restricted acceptable contrast ratio (30:1). A 20:1 contrast ratio inherent in the scene allows for extra contrast (modelling) added by lighting treatment.

29

Studio Cyclorama

The cyclorama (cyc) provides a general-purpose background. It can be used as a neutral or decorative staging facility, and introduced to create the illusion of space. It is usually in the form of a large taut 'cloth' which is suspended around the edge of the acting area. It is made of plastic, fireproofed duck, canvas or filled gauze and should be free of blemishes and, if possible, seam-free.

The height of the cyc is determined by the height of the studio and the type of production. For a 150 m² studio a suitable height for the cyc would be about 5 m (16 ft), but if production requirements are for long, wide-angle shots and/or low-angle shots, a higher cyc may be necessary. The cyc can be suspended by means of tapes tied at 0.3 m (1 ft) intervals to a scaffold pole suspension system, or by means of hooks on to runners using a special heavy-duty curtain track.

The mobile cyc

The second method, although more expensive, offers more flexibility in that the cyc can be moved easily. Also on the occasions when the cyc is not required it can be drawn together and conveniently stored on its rail in the studio. If double tracks are fitted, different coloured cloths can be quickly interchanged.

The cyc can either be allowed to hang freely in folds or, as is more usual, stretched taut. This is done by rolling up the spare cloth at the foot of the cyc and weighting it with stage weights or a suitably heavy scaffold pole, or by inserting an aluminium pole into a hemmed sleeve along the foot of the cyc.

Cyc colour

The most versatile colour for the cyc is off-white (60% reflectance) because it can be lit to any chosen colour by placing colour filters over the luminaires. With suitable four-colour lighting units (page 100) colour mixing over a wide range of hues and saturation can be achieved.

Additionally it is useful to have both black and chroma-key blue cycloramas. If these can be suspended on double tracks together with a white cyc, they can be interchanged quickly.

Rear-lit cyc

An alternative to using a front-lit cloth/plastic cyc is to use a translucent screen, rear-lit with dimmable high frequency fluorescent lights. The translucent screen can have its own inherent colour/design or the colour may be achieved using a mixture of coloured lights.

Care and storage

Great care should be taken if the cyc is removed from the studio. Avoid dampness—it produces stains. It should preferably be stored hanging up, not folded, because creases are difficult to remove when next the cyc is used. Even when the material is stretched taut, they persist for long periods

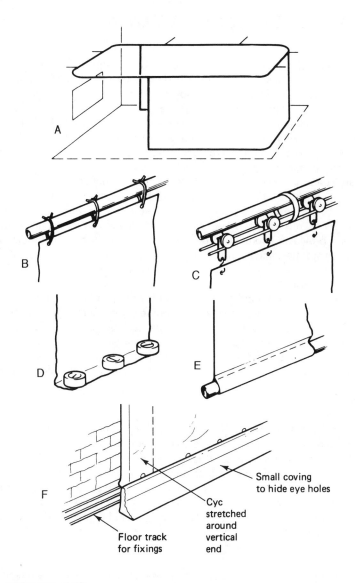

A

B

C

D

E

Small coving
to hide eye holes

Cyc
stretched
around
vertical
end

F

Floor track
for fixings

The cyclorama cloth

The acting area must *not* be completely enclosed by the cyc (A). A clear 'exit' must
be left for easy evacuation of the studio. The radius of the corners should be at least
1.6 m (5ft), ideally 2.7 m (9ft). The cloth may be simply tied onto a scaffold pole (B),
or may be suspended from a heavy-duty curtain track (C). Methods for stretching
the cyc cloth are: by weights holding surplus cloth taut (D); by a tubular scaffold
pole in a sleeve (E); using floor fixings and vertical 'stopper' (F), or simply a heavy
chain in the hem of the cyc.

Technical Equipment Store

Much of the technical equipment in a television studio is not required for every production. Studios are extremely busy places. Scenery needs to be erected, lamps rigged in their required positions, floors painted etc. Equipment left around in the studio constitutes a hazard for the rigging crews, wastes space and is itself at risk. Storage space outside the setting area is, therefore, essential. A room with large doors and direct access to the studio is desirable, so that it can also store the regularly used equipment, i.e. cameras and booms, picture monitors etc.

If a large enough storeroom is available, it is good practice at the end of the working day to move all the operational equipment not required for the same production the following day into this room, storing it in a tidy fashion and covering it with dust sheets where possible. In addition to the mobile studio equipment, provision should also be made for the storage of such items as isolating transformers and caption stands.

Lighting equipment
Lighting equipment presents a particular problem. Most lighting fittings and their accessories are bulky, heavy and cumbersome. Some can be left in readiness in the studio, but many others will be interchanged between the store and the studio for every production. A mobile storage rack should therefore be provided, with supporting rails for the luminaires, and with some provision for carrying sundry accessories (flags, colour medium holders, effects etc.).

Camera cables
Camera cables should always be coiled in a figure-of-eight fashion when stored on the floor, in order to avoid twisting the cable. Unfortunately, this wastes considerable floor space. It is useful, therefore, to have cable drums fitted to the walls, preferably on a spindle so that the camera cables can be wound on and off quickly. Other cables such as lighting and mains extension leads should be coiled up and stored on wall hooks. If it is not possible to provide individual hooks for the cables, each should be linen-taped together to avoid mutual entanglement.

General storage
Drawers and cupboards are useful for the general storage of smaller items. It is not, however, advisable to keep delicate or expensive equipment such as microphones in utility storage. Instead special precautions should be taken for their security and to protect them from accidental damage.

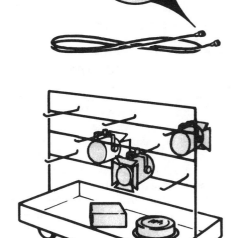

Pedestal safety
Where equipment is fitted with safety locks, these should be locked before storage. A safety chain on the camera head locks the tilting mechanism. A hook or turn-lock may prevent column movement.

Cable storage
Camera cables should be stored in a figure-of-eight pattern with dust covers fitted on both ends. Power and video cables should be stored on drums and wall hooks. (Discarded videotape spools make useful supports for storage of short cables.)

Storage trolley
A trolley should be available for movement of small items of equipment. Lighting equipment is more conveniently moved on a specially designed wheeled rack containing hooks for supporting the lights, and a tray for accessories.

Make-up

Make-up requirements vary from the corrective (such as lightening an obtrusive beard line, removing the shine from a bald head, normal presenter make-up) to a full character make-up which may involve ageing, scars, wigs, etc.

A room set aside specifically for make-up is desirable even in the smallest installation. It should be adjacent to the studio, well lit with good ventilation and maintained at a comfortable working temperature. A well-equipped make-up room not only enables the make-up specialist to work effectively with the precision this job entails but provides surroundings that staff and performers alike will find congenial.

Typical facilities
The figure opposite shows the typical facilities in a make-up area, in this case with one make-up position. Each position should have a washable working surface, ample leg room and a foot rest. The make-up chair, complete with head-rest, should be adjustable in height and preferably of the swivel type. There should be sufficient room to allow the make-up artist to work from either side of the chair. A large wall-mounted mirror is provided at each position with peripheral lighting. Flat lighting is desirable; this can be obtained with an arrangement of fluorescent tubes and diffusers. It is useful if these can be of the high frequency type to reduce the effects of flicker and have some form of dimming system.

In all except the smallest installations, hand basins with hairdressing equipment should be provided, as well as several power and razor sockets. Where appropriate, an area of work surface should be made available for wig dressing etc.

Storage should be provided for make-up materials, hairstyling equipment, razors, cleaning agents etc. Under E.C. safety legislation all hazardous substances must be stored in a locked metal cupboard and an assessment carried out of any safety implications.

Monitoring and communication
It is essential that the make-up area has a monitor feed with studio output, including sound, to ensure that the make-up staff and artistes keep up to date with the programme. Any corrective make-up required 'on set' can also be detected, but because the make-up monitor will probably not be of the highest quality it is always better to use the vision control monitors for proper assessment of make-up.

The make-up room should have a telephone extension and intercom with the studio, but preferably not be fitted with production talkback: not all the director's words may be for the performers' ears!

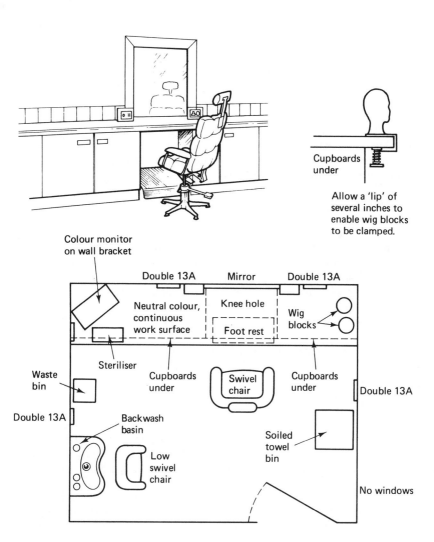

Cupboards under

Allow a 'lip' of several inches to enable wig blocks to be clamped.

Colour monitor on wall bracket

Double 13A   Mirror   Double 13A

Neutral colour, continuous work surface

Knee hole

Foot rest

Wig blocks

Steriliser

Cupboards under

Swivel chair

Cupboards under

Double 13A

Waste bin

Double 13A

Backwash basin

Soiled towel bin

Low swivel chair

No windows

Make-up area

Each make-up position should combine well-lit working conditions for the make-up artist, with comfort for the performer.

The make-up area should be designated a No Smoking area for safety reasons (flammable liquids) as well as for health reasons.

Floor covering: neutral colour, with a non-slip, washable surface.

Wall decoration: also a neutral colour.

Storage: cleaning fluids should be stored in a lockable cupboard. If productions involve plastic mouldings (prosthetics), materials must be kept in a refrigerator.

A notice must be available in the area listing the substances that have been assessed and approved for use.

35

Costume

The facilities required for costume or wardrobe purposes can vary considerably, according to the types of production being handled. In a small studio complex a large room is desirable in which to carry out the work of costume design, construction, fitting, correction and maintenance. It should be a room with natural daylight and preferably fitted with tungsten lighting. Fluorescent lighting if used, should be of high colour rendition (> 90) to avoid distortion of colour values. Also included should be hot/cold water supplies plus drainage and an ample supply of power sockets.

Typical facilities
The illustration shows the use of the working space in a room allocated for costume in a studio complex handling the full range of programmes but on a limited scale. A floor-standing steamer for suits, hats and large costumes can also be used in the studio for steaming creases out of drapes. A good variety of haberdashery is essential, as are basic cleaning materials; pure soap, methylated spirits and trichlorethane, in can and aerosol form, will save most accidents. Male and female tailor's dress stands are extremely useful; if on a tight budget use the small average sizes—they can always be padded-out to a larger size when needed. The overlocker or serger is invaluable, it can save so much time on otherwise labour-intensive tasks.

A Polaroid camera is a useful tool for making swift records for costume continuity purposes.

Costume suitability
Clothing may prove unsuitable on camera for technical or artistic reasons, e.g. too dark, appearing translucent, or with close regular patterns that produce distracting strobing effects. When the camera exposure is adjusted for good facial tones, costumes (e.g. shirts, blouses) which are too light or shiny will appear over-bright, or even reproduce as white areas with little detail.

The remedy is either to use off-white costumes or lightly dye the offending costume to overcome the problem. It is a good practice to encourage regular presenters to test all costumes 'on camera' before committing them to a programme.

Where chroma key is used in a production (see page 80) no costumes should be of a similar hue to the switching colour (e.g. blue) otherwise spurious effects will arise.

Monitoring and communication
Similar facilities to the make-up area should be included in the costume area, i.e. monitor with studio output plus sound, intercom and telephone.

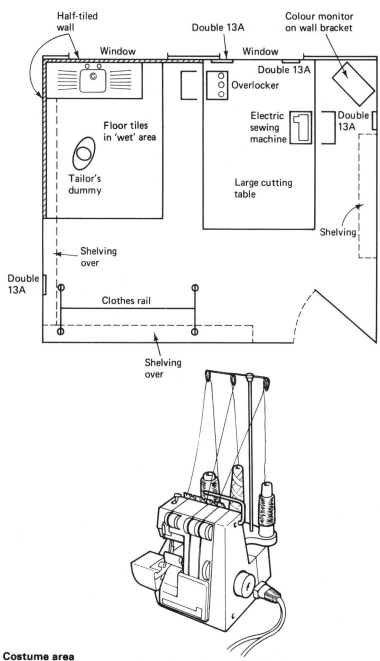

Half-tiled wall

Double 13A

Colour monitor on wall bracket

Window

Window

Double 13A

Overlocker

Floor tiles in 'wet' area

Electric sewing machine

Double 13A

Tailor's dummy

Large cutting table

Double 13A

Shelving

Shelving over

Double 13A

Clothes rail

Shelving over

Costume area

A typical layout is shown (top). A washing machine and tumble dryer are also needed, but these should be located in a separate area because they produce too much noise and heat. The overlocker (bottom) cuts and sews material in one operation, either single or multi-layer.

37

Equipment Maintenance Area

Although maintenance is of several distinct types (mechanical, electrical, electronic, plant etc.), a single general purpose servicing area close to the studio is the minimum requirement. It should have doors wide enough to permit access of bulky studio equipment and windows, if any, fitted with blinds. Laminated plastic working surfaces should be at a convenient height for staff to work either standing or seated on a stool. A generous number of power outlets should be provided at the rear of the bench. Sound and vision tie-lines from the studio carrying pulses and test signals, with some spare lines, are essential. Local extract ventilation (LEV) must be provided with particular attention to solder fumes which can be harmful.

Storage

Maintenance engineers are renowned hoarders of things which 'could come in useful'; thus, compromise has to be made between legroom and storage. Some drawers with labelled compartments for the storage of small electrical components are desirable so that they may be located quickly. Cables are usually stored on wall hooks.

A tool roll or box for small tools including screwdrivers, pliers etc. is also necessary. Larger tools may be kept in a drawer, though a preferred system is to hang them on a wall to enable a visual check to be kept. Each tool is allocated a hook over a painted silhouette of the tool. The bench should have a precision soldering station, a good quality vice and an illuminated desk magnifier. A filing cabinet for manuals, technical literature and fault records should be provided together with a plan chest for system diagrams etc.

Test equipment

Some items of electronic equipment are essential: a precision oscilloscope (with high gain and dual beam capability), a vectorscope, two multi-meters for simultaneous measurements and a variable power supply. For precision camera alignment a grey scale and a light meter are essential. For complex, miniaturised or digital equipment it may be cost-effective to ensure that manufacturers or suppliers can offer a maintenance back-up service rather than invest in sophisticated maintenance equipment and highly skilled staff. Modern equipment is very reliable yet complex, making fault finding difficult and time-consuming for an engineer who may not have an intimate knowledge of its design.

Lighting

In addition to conventional lighting there should be fluorescent lighting directly over the working surfaces together with adjustable table lamps. An inspection lamp or torch can also prove very useful.

Typical studio maintenance room

This general purpose maintenance room provides regular servicing facilities
(electrical, electronic, mechanical) for the small studio.

Furnishings include: (1) plastic-topped heavy-duty bench, (2) vari-height stool
with back support, (3) storage cupboards/drawers, (4) small component drawers,
(5) document filing cabinet, (6) adjustable wall lamp, (7) extensive power points.

Tools include: (8) large items on storage rack, (9) comprehensive portable tool
kit, (10) oscilloscope, (11) multimeter, (12) soldering iron with heat-shield stand
(a desoldering station is also required).

For safety, only qualified staff should use the area. An isolator near the door for
making the area electrically safe is essential, and local extract ventilation for
solder fumes should be provided.

Safety in the Studio

Safety is a very personal matter—the behaviour of the individual affects everyone. Safety is the result of anticipation, care and sensible regulations. It is a good policy to have someone specifically responsible for safety. Some studio hazards are detailed here, but always watch for others as well. Health and Safety at Work legislation must be observed.

Fire
This is a major subject in itself and the advice of the local fire authority is recommended when considering the many factors involved. All studios must comply with the local building regulations.

Large studios have a fire lane about one metre wide around the studio perimeter. This is a non-acting area and no equipment or scenery is allowed to remain in it. It provides unobstructed access to the studio exits. In the smaller studios this may not be entirely practical because of space lost, but there must always be unobstructed areas to two exits. Any actual fire used in the studio should be stringently supervised, with the fire-fighting apparatus at the ready.

Electrical
Special safety regulations have to be observed if more than one phase of the mains supply is present in the studio. This is because a high voltage exists (415 V for a 250 V supply or 400 V for a 230 V supply) between any two phases—and this can be *lethal*! All metalwork associated with electrical equipment should be earthed (grounded). All electrical equipment should be fitted with a correctly wired 3-core mains lead. Where domestic electrical equipment and musical instruments are fitted with a 2-wire mains lead, an isolating transformer should be used.

Safety bonds
Luminaires should be tightly clamped to the lighting suspension system, and must be fitted with wire safety bonds. All accessories (e.g. barndoors) must be safety bonded to the luminaire, unless they are captive.

Tripping accidents
The most common trip is over cables on the floor. All cables crossing main access 'lanes' to the studio exits should have portable cable ramps over them.

Lifting
Staff with back troubles abound in television studios. All staff should be given adequate training on how to lift correctly. If possible staff should be given first aid training including artificial resuscitation.

Unstable items
It is all too easy to rest a ladder against a wall, inadequately support a scenic flat, raise a heavy lamp high on an unweighted lighting stand. But the unguarded moment will come, when the unstable hazard falls—pulled by a cable perhaps—and then it is too late to think about SAFETY!

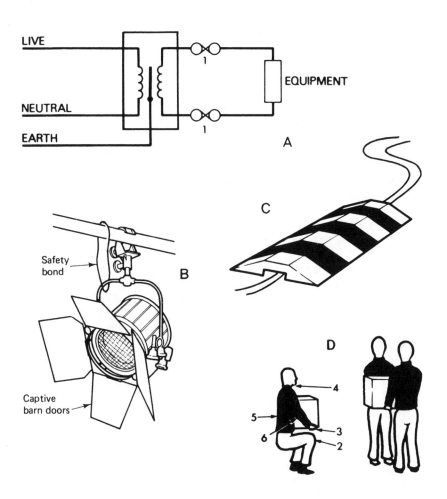

LIVE

NEUTRAL

EARTH

EQUIPMENT

A

C

Safety bond

B

Captive barn doors

D

A. Isolating transformer
The isolating transformer prevents the possibility of electrical shock from equipment-to-earth contact. Its case and electrostatic screen must be earthed. The secondary winding must not be earthed, and must have correctly rated fuses (1) in each leg.

B. Safety bonds
Wire safety bonds should be fitted to all suspended and overhead equipment. Luminaires and their attachments are bonded as we see here.

C. Cable-ramp
This typical cable-ramp (cover) in wood or glass-fibre, about a metre (3 ft) long, protects cables and prevents trip-over accidents.

D. Weight handling
Get into the habit of lifting objects safely. (2) Knees bent, (3) palm grip (not just fingers), (4) chin in, (5) straight back, (6) elbows in. If the object is heavy, get assistance.

41

The Vision System

The colour TV system is based on the principle that with three suitable primary colours of light (red, green and blue) it is possible to reproduce white and a gamut of colours. The precise 'colour' one sees depends on the relative amounts of red, green and blue light.

In colour television the display tube on the colour monitor generates three separate red, green and blue (RGB) pictures, which produce an appropriate mixture at any point on the screen, and the viewer sees a particular colour. It is the colour camera's function to derive the appropriate RGB signals which eventually feed to the display. Colour cameras use a light-splitting system behind the zoom lens; this splits the light into red, green and blue light, which is then focused onto the appropriate camera tube or CCD imager as an optical image of the scene to be televised.

Scanning

The optical image is converted by the sensor into an electrical charge pattern which is 'read out' or 'scanned' in a regular pattern to produce an electrical signal. In the UK the scanning process operates at 625 lines/picture; in the USA it operates at 525 lines. The picture rate is repeated at 25 pictures/second for the UK and 30 pictures/second for the USA; this is to ensure that the displayed picture is seen as a continuous picture and not as a scanning spot.

Interlace

By scanning first the odd lines of the picture and then the even lines (interlacing) the effective picture rate is doubled, and flicker is significantly reduced. This is known as interlaced scanning.

Coding

To avoid having to transmit three separate video signals (RGB), they are coded into one composite signal. This conveys both brightness information (luminance signal, indicated by the symbol Y) and colour information (chrominance signal, consisting of R-Y and B-Y). There are three basic *incompatible* systems for coding: NTSC, PAL and SECAM.

Colour picture monitors respond to both parts of the signal, while monochrome monitors extract only the brightness (luminance) information.

To ensure that the picture on the monitor is displayed in perfect synchronism with the cameras' scanning process, synchronising pulses are added to the coded signal in the coder.

Bandwidth

The video system must be capable of reproducing fine detail in a picture. This represents an extremely high-frequency signal, greater than five million cycles per second (5 MHz) when using a 625-line system. All parts of the vision system must therefore be capable of handling a wide bandwidth of frequencies, from 50 Hz to 5 MHz; this illustrates one of the cost problems of vision systems. (An audio system, by comparison, involves a bandwidth of 30 Hz to 16 kHz.)

42

Additive colour mixing

The basic principle of additive mixing can be represented by a colour triangle.
Red, green and blue are the *primary colours;* magenta, cyan and yellow are
the *complementary* or *secondary colours.*

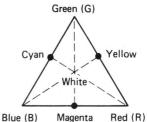

Green + Red produces Yellow
Blue + Green produces Cyan
Blue + Red produces Magenta

Green + Magenta produces White
Red + Cyan produces White
Blue + Yellow produces White

Overview of the camera

Most lightweight combined camera-recorders record the 'component' signals.

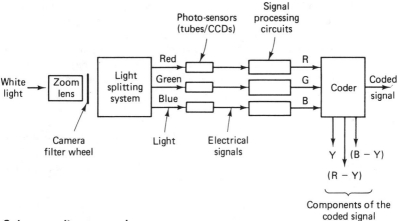

Colour monitor processing

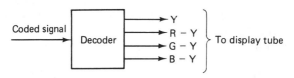

The colour monitor has a decoder which is able to derive the G-Y signal as well
as the 'components'; these are then used to control the brightness of the
appropriate colour phosphor on the tube, i.e., (R-Y)-Y=R signal.

43

Choice of Camera System

A wide range of camera systems is available, and it is important to select an appropriate type. The design of small lightweight cameras has developed rapidly, with continual improvement in performance and reduction in weight. Such cameras obviously offer great flexibility, both in the studio and on location. They can be hand-held and are easily rigged/de-rigged. Most can have supplementary accessories added when required for off-shoulder working, i.e. larger viewfinder, matte box, larger zoom lenses, servo zoom controls. Portable video cameras can be used with a separate videotape recorder or incorporate the VTR within the camera unit. Which type you use will affect your editing requirements.

Large heavy cameras with full facilities, although capable of producing excellent pictures, will not give you the same flexibility in use; generally their use is restricted to studio productions and coverage of location events, i.e. sport, religious services etc. They will of course be more expensive and require heavier mountings.

Composite/component
Formerly, the complete composite video signal was recorded, incorporating both the luminance information (Y) and the colour (chrominance) information. Current videotape systems record the luminance information and colour information separately. This is known as component recording and is used in combined camera/recorders, and other systems, with superior results. Your videotape editing facilities must be compatible with the system you are using. Component signals are also used in digital devices and in digital recorders. Generally, all new stations will be component engineered (analogue) or operate with a digital component system.

Remote control
Except for ENG type purposes it is extremely useful for the camera system to have remote control of normal vision control functions (see page 62). This is invaluable for consistently high quality pictures, essential for ensuring that the edited programme has well-matched shots.

Camera sensitivity (page 90)
Most Japanese manufacturers quote the camera sensitivity with reference to a special luminance, i.e. a surface of 90% reflectivity. To obtain a comparison of relative sensitivity this must be converted to an equivalent sensitivity for a 60% reflectivity (TV white) and at the 'nominal' lens aperture for the particular camera. For example, 2000 lux at f/5.6 with 90% Peak White becomes 3000 lux at f/5.6 with 60% Peak White and 375 lux at f/2.0 (nominal aperture for 2/3 inch format).

The signal/noise ratio should also be quoted when stating sensitivity and used when comparing relative sensitivities of camera systems.

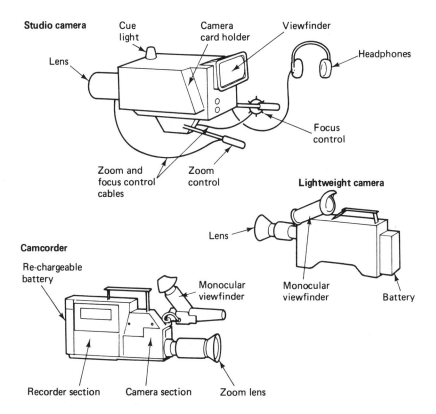

Studio camera — Cue light — Camera card holder — Viewfinder — Headphones — Lens — Focus control — Zoom and focus control cables — Zoom control

Lightweight camera — Lens — Monocular viewfinder — Battery

Camcorder — Re-chargeable battery — Monocular viewfinder — Recorder section — Camera section — Zoom lens

Note: lightweight cameras may be converted for studio operation with external power supply, large viewfinder etc., at additional cost.

Simple facilities
Extremely portable, small and lightweight.
Battery/mains operated, low power consumption.
Sensitive.
Small viewfinder.
Simple servo control on zoom lens.
Automatic line-up.
Auto-iris.
Includes two microphone circuits.

Full facilities
Basic body of camera may still be small and lightweight.
Large viewfinder.
Usually mains operated, large power consumption.
Sensitive.
Larger, better quality lens, superior servo controls on lens.
Automatic line-up.
Auto-iris.
Remote control of vision control facilities.
Cue lights.
Talkback/reverse talkback.
Viewfinder mix facility.

Picture Generation

Sensor system: Tube/CCD

The charge coupled device (CCD) is a solid-state device which has rapidly replaced the conventional camera pick-up tube (Plumbicon and Saticon). Both the CCD and the camera tube use a light-sensitive material which changes its resistance when light falls on it (photo-conductive). The optical image on the sensor therefore results in an electrical charge pattern being formed which is processed in the camera to produce the video signal. The CCD is a special integrated-circuit and is often referred to as a 'chip' camera.

Camera configuration

Video cameras may use either a single device to generate the video signal, or a three-path system.

Single-sensor cameras. These use a single device to convert the relative brightness of an optical image into three electrical signals, by putting a grill consisting of red, green and blue filter stripes over the face of the sensor. The image is thus split into the three required primary colours which are detected and processed by the camera to produce a colour video signal with no colour fringing problems. This type of camera does not work too well under low light levels and does not resolve fine detail very well. It costs much less than the three-sensor camera, and has considerable merit for closed-circuit television applications, or for news 'stringers'.

Three-sensor cameras. Red, green and blue optical images are obtained by using a system of prisms and special filters (dichroic filters). The three separate images are converted in the electrical signals RGB which are used to produce the video signals for recording purposes (i.e. composite or component). Professional cameras all use three-sensor systems, the picture quality being far superior to the single-sensor system. Three-tube cameras have the disadvantage that unless the three electrical images are identical in size and shape the synthesised image on the colour monitor will have colour fringes. The registration of the three images is an important feature to check on any camera specification. Three-CCD cameras do not suffer from this problem as the chips are factory set to extreme accuracy, and are cemented into place on the surfaces of the light-splitting block.

Resolution

The ability to resolve fine detail in a televised scene is a measure of the 'resolution' of the camera. The resolution performance of a tube camera is determined by the tube characteristics and scanning system; the Saticon has slightly better resolution than the Plumbicon tube. The resolution of a chip camera is limited by the number of pixels on the chip. Advances have produced chips with over 700 pixels in the horizontal direction.

CCD vs tube cameras

The CCD camera has rapidly replaced the tube camera for most applications, for the following reasons:

Ease of operation
- Smaller and lighter in weight.
- Uses less power.
- No warm-up needed.
- Minimum of technical alignment, fewer controls.
- No registration needed.
- No lag or burn-in effects on highlights.
- Less light required, approx. one *f*-stop more sensitive.

Robustness
- Very rugged construction.
- Not affected by vibration—no microphony.
- Not affected by external fields—electric or magnetic.
- CCD does not have limited life like tubes.
- Very reliable in operation.
- Cheaper to operate.
- Operates within temperature range $-20°C$ to $+45°C$.

Performance
- Good signal/noise ratio, better than 60 dB.
- Excellent dynamic range.
- Good colorimetry (with infra-red filter).
- Good dynamic resolution—less blurring on moving objects.
- Resolution determined by number of pixels (currently better than 700 pixels horizontally enabling 700 lines/picture to be resolved).
- Vertical smear, a CCD effect where *extreme* highlights produce a vertical line, usually red in colour; this is eliminated in the Frame Transfer CCD and reduced to an insignificant level in the Frame Interline Transfer CCD. Smear is a characteristic of the Interline Transfer CCD, but it must be remembered that it only occurs on an extreme overload, i.e. greater than five-stop overload ($\times 32$).
- Geometry of CCD sensors is inherently good, however any geometric distortion in the lens will be difficult to correct. CCD cameras therefore require good quality lenses.

47

Camera Lenses

The function of the camera lens is to produce the best possible optical image of the scene to be televised on the camera sensor system (tube or CCD). The lens is the first stage in the production of a good quality television picture, so great care should be taken in choosing the right one; not only for its basic optical properties, i.e. focal length and maximum aperture, but also for its quality of optical performance, i.e. resolution, image contrast, etc.

The lens will be of fixed focal length or, more likely, of variable focal length—a zoom lens. The pre-occupation with lens focal length is because the angle of view of the lens and hence the size of the shot is related to its focal length.

Focal length and angle of view (horizontal)
The focal length of a lens, usually quoted in millimetres, gives an indication of its 'bending' power. A short focal length lens produces a wide angle of view of the scene, whereas a long focal length lens gives a narrow angle of view (a close-up shot). The precise angle of view for a given lens depends not only on its focal length but also on the width of the active sensor area. For production planning purposes it is more useful to use the horizontal angle of view than focal length.

Lens aperture
All lenses are fitted with a variable iris mechanism known as the lens aperture. This is used to control the amount of light passed by the lens. The focal length and the diameter of the lens aperture are related by the concept of f-number. All lenses at the same f-number will give the same exposure provided the transmission factors of the lenses are identical. Obviously, lenses with large physical apertures (and small f-numbers) will result in a greater camera sensitivity; unfortunately when lenses are opened up to a very wide aperture the quality of the images suffers (loss of sharpness), so usually a compromise has to be achieved. The 'depth of field', the range of subject distances within acceptable focus, also decreases with decrease in f-number.

Zoom lens
This has a continuously variable focal length over a given range. Zoom lenses are usually specified as a product of zoom ratio and minimum focal length, e.g. 14 × 9 means that the zoom ratio is 14:1 and the minimum focal length is 9 mm. The maximum focal length is therefore 14 × 9 = 126 mm. The lens manufacturer will also quote the angle of view for a given lens, in the above case 52°:4° when designed for use with 18 mm sensor format size.

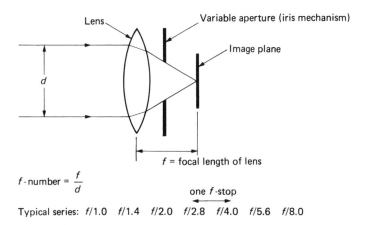

$f\text{-number} = \dfrac{f}{d}$

f = focal length of lens

one f-stop

Typical series: $f/1.0$ $f/1.4$ $f/2.0$ $f/2.8$ $f/4.0$ $f/5.6$ $f/8.0$

'Opening up' ◄─────────────── ────────► 'Stopping down'

Lens aperture
Opening up the lens by one f-stop will double the exposure.

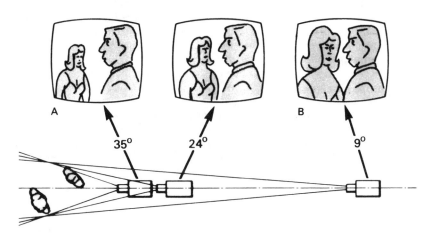

Using a zoom lens
Pre-focus the lens by zooming in to the subject, focus, then zoom out to the desired shot size and framing. The zoom should remain in focus on a pre-focused subject distance throughout its zoom range. This is called zoom tracking; see page 58.

Perspective and the lens
The apparent depth in a picture (perspective) changes with camera position. For a given size of foreground subject, note how the wide-angle lens (A) exaggerates the distance, while the narrow-angle lens (B) compresses the perspective.
The range of subject distances within acceptable focus is called the depth of field; it is directly proportional to the f-number but varies as the square of the lens angle and subject distance.

Choice of Lens

Generally a manufacturer will increase the narrow-angle end of the zoom range as the zoom ratio is increased, e.g. 12 × 9, 14 × 9, 17 × 9. It may seem that the best lens to go for would be the 17 × 9; however, the larger the ratio, the larger the lens and the greater the cost and weight factor. Large ratio zooms are more useful for outside broadcast work than studio but difficult to hand-hold at the narrow-angle end of the range. The weight of the lens is also a factor to consider for hand-held cameras.

Ultra-wide angle zoom lenses are available, but with restricted ratio, typically 8 × 6, this has a maximum angle of view of 72.5° and a short minimum object distance (0.3 m).

Minimum object distance
A zoom lens will have a limit on how close one can go to the subject and still maintain focus. This is known as the minimum object distance (MOD). To avoid this becoming a limitation make sure that you purchase zoom lenses with an MOD to suit your requirements, e.g. 0.7 m or less for studio work.

Macro
The macro facility allows the camera to be used at extremely short object distances by using the rear element to focus (instead of the front element). This is particularly useful for close-ups of small objects or fine detail, but note that when using macro the zoom lens will no longer 'track' (page 60).

Maximum lens aperture
This should be at least one stop open on the nominal aperture (page 91).

Range extenders
A useful facility on a zoom is a range extender whereby operating a small lever causes the range to change but not the *ratio*, e.g. 9–126 mm × 2 becomes 18–252 mm. Under these circumstances the *f*-number doubles resulting in a decrease in exposure by 2 stops. Range extenders also magnify any residual lens defects, i.e. degrade picture quality.

Servos
The focus and zoom controls can be manually operated or servo controlled. The advantage of a servo system is smoother control; it also allows a 'shot box' facility whereby several shot sizes can be pre-set and recalled at the push of a button. A further advantage of the servo is that it enables a camera to be remotely operated, e.g. in a simple presentation area with no camera person.

Servo systems designed for studio operation usually offer much smoother control than the basic servos designed for ENG type operation.

The iris can be manually or servo controlled. The servo mode allows the iris to be remotely controlled or operated on 'auto-iris'. In the latter case the exposure is determined automatically by the camera electronics.

Typical portable camera lens specification for different camera applications

	Normal	Wide angle	Narrow angle
Zoom designation	14×8	8×6	18×8.5
Zoom ratio	14:1	8:1	18:1
Focal length	8–112 mm	6–48 mm	8.5–153 mm
with range extender×2	16–224 mm	12–96 mm	17–306 mm
Angle of view	57.6°–4.5°	72.5°–9°	54.7°–3.3°
with range extender	30.8°–2.3°	36°–4.5°	29.0°–1.6°
Maximum f-number	f/1.7 (8–91 mm)	f/1.7 (6–33 mm)	f/1.7 (8.5–113 mm)
	f/2.1 (112 mm)	f/1.9 (48 mm)	f/2.3 (153 mm)
with range extender	f/3.4 (16–182 mm)	f/3.4 (12–66 mm)	f/3.4 (17–226 mm)
	f/4.2 (224 mm)	f/3.8 (96 mm)	f/4.6 (306 mm)
MOD	0.7 m	0.3 m	0.9 m
Weight	2.4 kg	1.7 kg	1.59 kg
Macro	Yes	Yes	Yes

Normal   Normal studio and location work with a short MOD.

Wide angle   Usually more useful for location work, operating in confined spaces, candid shots, following subjects, operating close to subjects (without getting other people between camera and subject), has a very short MOD.

Narrow angle Useful when operating at longer subject distances than normal. With ×2 range extender this is a useful lens, but beware of zoom ramping. (When using the long focal length end of the zoom range at maximum aperture there will usually be a reduction in the effective f-number, typically for ratios greater than 12:1. This effect, known as zoom ramping, is caused by the front element of the zoom acting as the limiting aperture.)

Maximum camera sensitivity (Without added electronic gain)

Note the high sensitivity of the modern CCD cameras.

14 x 8 lens with $\frac{2}{3}$ inch CCD camera

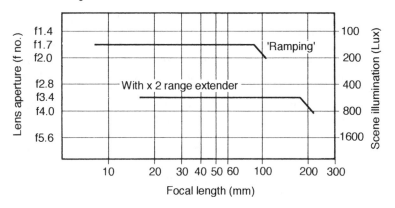

Camera Mountings

A firm camera support is essential for steady shots. A good mounting permits smooth shot development over a wide range of camera heights and angles.

Tripod
This is a three-legged stand with independent adjustment of the length of each leg. The tripod is cheap and light. With the addition of a wheeled based (skid) the 'rolling tripod' can be easily moved, but only out of vision if optimum smoothness is required. Some have an adjustable centre column that permits changes in camera height, but only out of vision (see page 183).

Pedestal
This is a sophisticated, one-person camera mounting, enabling both subtle and marked changes in camera position and height to be made on shot. It can be moved around the studio quickly and silently, with minimum effort, guided by a steering-ring or tiller. The weight of camera and panning-head is counterbalanced, thus enabling the cameramen to change elevation easily. Inside the pedestal base, mechanical linkages line up its three wheels, either to point in the same direction (crab) or to enable one to steer whilst the others follow. Great care must be taken to secure the central column before attempting to remove a camera. This lock must not then be removed whilst the column is in its 'low' position because it will spring up with enormous force.

Pan and tilt head
A good pan and tilt head mounted between the camera and the main support is essential. A well-engineered head securely holds the camera, preserves near perfect balance whatever the tilt position and has adjustable friction to facilitate the smoothest possible motion. A lock secures the head if unattended.

Sophisticated mountings
Motorised mountings requiring two or more operators are available for a greater range of shots but are generally unsuitable for small studios. Lightweight non-motorised versions that support a portable camera at the end of a counterbalanced jib arm, are very useful (see page 183). When choosing a studio camera mounting look for firm support, smooth pan and tilt action with adjustable friction, good counterbalance for the camera at any tilt angle and smooth manoeuvrability in vision.

For studios primarily used for interviews and discussions remote controlled camera heads may be worth considering, thus not requiring camera persons, though the remote functions can be overridden when they are required. Cameras must be in the optimum position. Shots can be memorised and recalled when required. Full robotics automate pedestal movement as well but this is expensive and requires careful planning. Except for use in some news operations this has not become widely used.

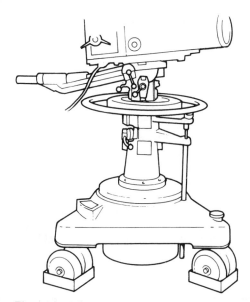

The pedestal

This typical studio pedestal (the Tern) is a lightweight pedestal suitable for the lighter colour camera. It can be easily handled and transported for location work on reasonably level floors.

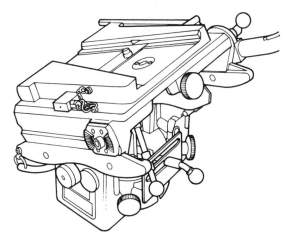

The pan and tilt head

This camera head (the Vinten Mark 7) is suitable for the lighter studio camera. The roller bearing and cam system, visible on the side, ensures good camera balance at any angle and the lubricated friction type of drag enables smooth camera movements with light pressure on the pan bar. Up to 60° of tilt angle is possible, depending on the type of camera employed. (See also lightweight cameras on pages **182/183**)

53

Camera Cables and Cabling Points

Unless operating a camera/recorder there is a need to connect the camera-head to its camera control unit and hence to the switcher and videotape recorder, or simply to connect the output of a camera to a portable videotape recorder. In the latter case the connecting cable will need to carry the vision signal from the camera, possibly a sound signal, remote start/stop signals for VTR, and a reverse vision circuit. With a 'full facilities' camera the cable will also include circuits for talkback, cue lights, synchronising pulses, power, control facilities etc. This is achieved either with a multi-core cable or tri-axial cable. The multi-core cable must be used with great care, because it is expensive and can be damaged easily. The systems using a tri-axial cable (a coaxial cable with an extra outer screen) have the advantage of a slimmer cable, lighter than multi-core, more robust and relatively cheap. However, they have the complication of requiring a special coding system to enable all the facilities to be provided along what is virtually a single circuit.

Cable care

If the camera cable is to be disconnected and stored, even for a few days, it is essential to fit its protective caps over each end to prevent dirt or moisture entering the socket-end or pins being bent at the plug-end. If caps are not available, cable ends should be wrapped in clean cloth and taped up.

Damage to the camera cable-end or to the entry socket on a television camera may occur if the cable is clamped to the pedestal body and the camera head then elevated with insufficient slack cable.

This form of damage can also occur with a clamped camera cable if the panning head is turned continuously in one direction and the camera cable becomes snarled up around the column of the pedestal.

Similarly, a cable should not be made to follow acute bends or twists in use because, if it is subsequently pulled tight, damage to the internal wires can result.

When the pedestal plus camera are pushed away to the side of the studio for storage at the end of the studio day, the cable should be coiled up in a figure-of-eight configuration alongside the camera.

Cabling points

The camera cable plugs into a cabling point on the studio wall. Alternative points are generally distributed around three or four studio walls. Some well-equipped studios have more cabling points than studio cameras. This enables each camera to route its cable to meet the production requirements of a particular programme, and so avoid long loops of straggling cable around the studio floor.

The cable end

The camera cable is fitted with a plug at either end, housing many small pin connections (1). Take care when attaching the cable, to avoid bending pins. Also ensure that the cable is pushed fully home and screwed up firmly.

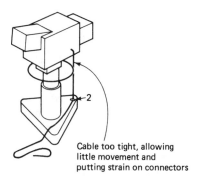

Cable too tight, allowing little movement and putting strain on connectors

Cable care

Anticipate possible cable damage by allowing sufficient cable length for column elevation and panning movements. Cable clamps (2) are usually fitted to the camera mounting.

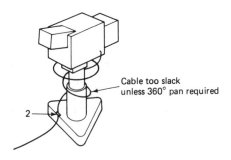

Cable too slack unless 360° pan required

Cable plugging

In small interview studios the cameras are connected to their CCUs through dedicated wall sockets. In larger studios camera cables plug into distribution boxes located at intervals along studio walls. These sockets are permanently routed to a communal patch panel (with point locations) near the camera control units. Here, flexible cables from these units plug into their associated camera's wallpoint link.

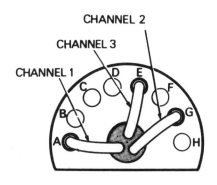

CHANNEL 2

CHANNEL 3

CHANNEL 1

Vision and Lighting Control Area

This area has two interrelated functions. Here the picture quality is continually monitored and adjusted by the vision operator, or video engineer (page 62) and here also the lighting facilities are controlled (page 108). Because these jobs require close co-ordination, the vision control desk and the lighting control panel (lighting console) should always be arranged side by side, preferably sharing common picture monitors. Optimum results cannot be achieved if they are located and operated in separate rooms.

Control room position
It is normal practice in smaller studio centres, where space is at a premium, to house the vision/lighting control area in a communal production control room, with the director and other programme staff. Such an arrangement has certain economies, but where space permits (page 18), a separate adjacent room with a communicating glass panel has advantages.

All the associated electronic equipment for the studio should be rack-mounted with adequate front and rear access in a room immediately adjacent to the production control area. If space is particularly restricted, this vision equipment may have to be placed in the production control area, but such an arrangement does not make for optimum servicing efficiency. Over-communal layouts can cause the different activity requirements to impinge on each other.

Cabling
Where a studio is purpose-built, false floors are preferred for control areas, for beneath them accessible cable ducts can house all power and video supplies. Similarly, ducting may be provided around the edges of the studio floor for camera cables, etc. If equipment has to be installed in an existing building, overhead trunking suspended from the ceiling can neatly and effectively solve difficult cabling problems.

Operational considerations
The positioning and layout of operational controls needs to be carefully considered. Equipment detail will be determined by manufacturers' design, but we should always bear in mind that operators will need to reach controls comfortably and quickly over long periods with a minimum of fatigue. There must be an uninterrupted view of all picture monitors, which should be arranged to permit both overall assessment and local scrutiny. The lighting control panel should also be conveniently located. It is often forgotten that adequate desk space is needed for production paperwork, such as scripts, cuesheets, lighting plots, etc.

In small studio productions, one person can handle both the studio lighting balance and operate vision controls. Larger productions require separate operators for lighting and picture control.

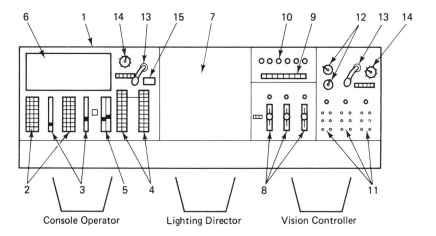

Lighting preview	Tx colour		Vision control PV mono	Vision control PV col
		Cam 1 mono	Cam 2 mono	Cam 3 mono

Monitor stack

Console Operator   Lighting Director   Vision Controller

Lighting and vision control room

This shows a typical layout. The numbers of staff are dictated by the scale of the operation. Smaller studios may combine the roles of lighting director and console operator; more basic set-ups may combine all three roles and even house the facilities in the production control room. Some broadcast studios have extra seating for an engineer (to monitor colour balance during recordings), for make-up and costume staff.

Facilities include lighting console (1) with lamp selection (2) and associated faders (3). Lamp brightness settings may be memorised in memory stores (4) and cross-fades between stores controlled by the sliders (5). A mimic (6) lists all the studio lights and their status, i.e. on/off, the selected memory file. Space is available on the desk for the lighting plot (7). The vision controller has the camera joysticks (8), test signals (9) and brightness and contrast of the monitors (10) under his control. An additional panel for fine camera colour balance (11) and TARIF control of telecine (12) is provided. Communications (13), monitoring (14) and a current load meter complete the layout.

57

Signal Processing
(Camera Control Unit)

The three signals, RGB, derived from the camera sensors require electronic processing before they are coded to provide the camera output signal. Modern cameras house all the processing electronics and the coder in the camera head, with some provision for remote control of important facilities. Older cameras carried out this signal processing in a separate camera control unit (CCU).

Control features

Typically the processing, mentioned in the manufacturer's literature, includes:

● *Detail enhancement*—special high-frequency correction used to improve the rendition of fine detail. It should be used with care: if over-corrected the pictures will look 'edgy' and artificially sharp, faces will look leathery in appearance due to the enhancement of spots, blemishes, skin pores etc. Noise is increased by detail enhancement.

● *Black-level adjustment (lift)*—used to establish the black level in a picture. In lightweight cameras this should be an automatic function.

● *Gamma correction*—the display tube has a non-linear law (see opposite). To compensate for this the RGB signals are pre-distorted in the camera to produce an overall effect which is approximately linear. Occasionally, gamma correction is used as an operational control to change the 'law' of the camera, i.e. to stretch or crush the dark areas of the picture. Stretching the dark areas will also increase the noise.

● *Iris*—remote control of the iris is essential to good vision control. It should be carefully adjusted to ensure correct exposure of the scene. Auto-iris should only be used on lightweight cameras when it is impossible to operate the iris, e.g. following rapid action between many areas the camera operator is preoccupied with framing and focus.

● *Gain (master gain)*—provides an increase in amplification to the video signal when operating in low-light conditions. Usually it is provided as switched increases in gain, e.g. a 6 dB increase in gain will double the signal level, equivalent to opening up the iris by one stop. Unfortunately, any increase in gain is accompanied by an increase in noise. When *white balancing* the cameras, the individual gain controls on the R and B channels will be adjusted to match signal levels with the G channel. This is usually an automatic facility on modern cameras. See page 60.

● *Linear matrix*—the deficiencies of the colour analysis by the light-splitting block and pick-up devices, can be compensated for by a small amount of coupling between the RGB signals. This improves the colour rendition of the camera.

The CCU originates appropriate control voltages and scanning signals for the camera sensors. Remote control panels are grouped together for ease of vision control and line-up.

Basic block diagram of a colour camera channel

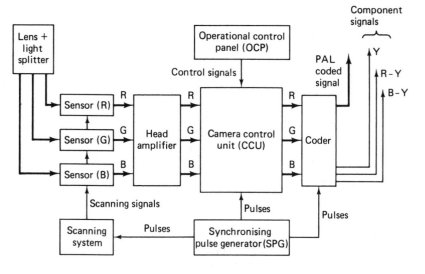

Need for contrast law correction (gamma correction)

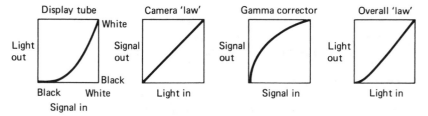

The linear camera law is modified by the gamma corrector to take account of the non-linear response of the display tube; this results in an approximately linear relationship between 'light into camera' and 'light out from display'.

Typical switched gain settings

Switched gain	Single device cameras	3-device cameras
1	+6 dB (equivalent to opening up by 1 stop)	+9 dB (equivalent to opening up by 1½ stops)
2	+12 dB (equivalent to opening up by 2 stops)	+18 dB (equivalent to opening up by 3 stops)

Because all forms of correction introduce extra noise on the signals it is usual for manufacturers to specify the signal-to-noise (S/N) ratio with all correction switched out, i.e. a 'flat' channel with gamma correction off, detail enhancement off, linear matrix out etc.

59

Line-up of Camera Channels

Camera performance tends to change with time and temperature, so periodic re-adjustments are necessary to restore it to a standard condition and avoid colour quality variations during a production. These 'line-up' readjustments may be carried out manually, semi-automatically, or entirely automatically.

To achieve consistently good pictures from a television camera, line-up is required. Modern lightweight cameras need little adjustment on a day-to-day basis, but do need to be white-balanced *every* time they are switched on. This is achieved by pointing the camera at a piece of white card illuminated by the same colour of light as that being used to illuminate the scene. Switching the camera to WHITE BALANCE causes its electronics to automatically achieve a neutral white output. With modern studio cameras line-up is also automatic, though some minor adjustments may be necessary.

Starting the day

It is better to ensure that camera channels, along with other vision equipment, are switched on for at least half an hour before they are required. This allows the electronics to stabilise before any adjustments are made. The amount of line-up required depends upon the type of camera in use; however, time should be allowed for this important operation.

CCD cameras require neither electronic focus nor registration. Older tube cameras will need 'registering' (setting the scan size and position of the images produced by each of the three tubes) and 'focusing' (an electronic rather than optical adjustment of each tube), on a regular basis. Registering of single-tube cameras is not required, although electronic focusing is.

Zoom tracking

Zoom lenses should remain in focus on a pre-focused subject throughout their zoom range. To check, zoom into a tight shot of an object. Focus the lens, then zoom out to the widest angle; the image should still be sharply focused. If not, the zoom tracking is out. To adjust this, the lens manufacturers' instructions should be followed. Large studio cameras should be checked before every recording or transmission.

Line-up charts

There are several types of chart available. Generally two will be needed. One has a series of white vertical and horizontal lines against a black background for registration purposes. The other consists of a grey scale step wedge against a neutral background to set the overall white balance of the camera (if it does not have an auto adjustment) and to set the exposure limits. Each camera in use should be pointed at the grey scale in turn, and small adjustments to the colour balance made to ensure that the cameras exactly match one another. The chart should be evenly illuminated with the same colour light as that in use in the studio.

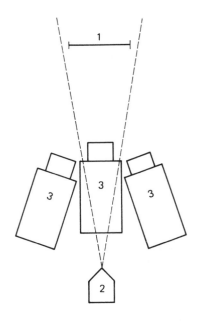

Camera line-up

The line-up chart (1) is evenly illuminated by the light (2), carefully adjusted to a specific illumination of the chart and colour temperature (usually 3000 K or just under). The cameras (3) should view the chart as orthogonally as possible.

Line-up charts

For tube cameras only: Registration chart to superimpose the images from the three tubes. Some cameras have automatic functions such as centring, black level and white level (for correct grey scale).

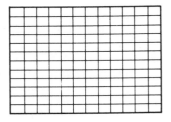

For all cameras: grey scale (vertical stripes in even steps of grey from black to white) to ensure that the combined red, green and blue outputs of the camera accurately reproduce the grey scale with no colour cast across any part of the scale.

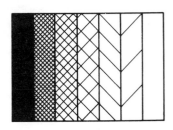

61

Vision Control

It is important that the cameras are adjusted to produce the best possible pictures for each shot, and also to ensure that the shots match from camera to camera and from shot to shot, e.g. face tones look the same. This is the basic function of vision control.

Lightweight cameras
Lightweight cameras usually have auto-white balance, auto-black level and auto-iris facilities, three of the main areas of interest for vision control. It should be remembered that the auto-iris control can give rise to errors when the camera is presented with scenes containing large areas of excessive highlights, e.g. white clouds. Ideally the camera operator should adjust the lens iris manually to suit each shot, using the viewfinder to judge the correct exposure.

Full-facility vision control
Cameras equipped with remote control of camera processing (such as iris, black level, gamma correction, fine detail enhancement, and colour correction in highlight and black areas) will enable the vision controller to achieve greater precision in control of picture quality and ensure that the pictures match one shot to the next. This is important even when shooting 'single camera'. At the beginning of rehearsal the camera iris should be set to its nominal value (see page 91) and the lighting levels balanced to achieve a satisfactory picture. Minor adjustments to iris and black level are made subsequently to ensure picture matching. Some shots may require more or less fine detail correction, which should be adjusted shot by shot. Any colour cast introduced by reflection of light from costumes or the set can be removed by means of the colour correction controls, and similarly for any variation in the colour temperature (whiteness) of the light sources used for each scene. Alternatively, the vision controller can deliberately introduce a colour cast, and produce warm pictures or cool pictures to match the mood of the scene as appropriate.

Further duties of the vision control engineer include camera line-up, the checking of all vision sources routed to the switcher, alignment of all the picture monitors in the studio control complex, and as a liaison point for camera crew when technical problems arise.

The vision controller works very closely with the lighting director, and in a small studio these duties may well be handled by one person.

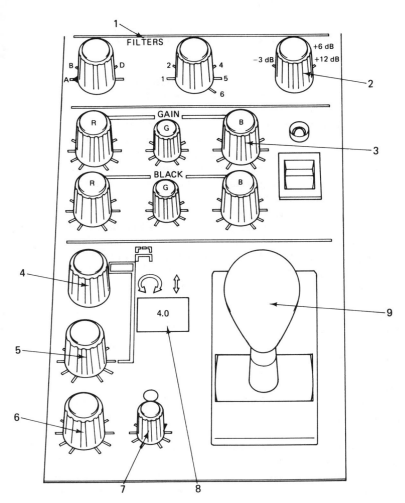

Vision control

This is a typical operational control panel (OCP) for a full-facilities camera.

1. Remote control of filter wheels located between lens and light-splitting system (colour correction, neutral density and effects filters).
2. Master gain control; extra gain is used when operating in low light.
3. Gain and black trims, used for minor adjustment of colour gain and black level when matching pictures.
4. Auto/manual iris control.
5. Detail enhancement.
6. Contrast control, used to modify the 'law', i.e. to stretch/crush appropriate parts of the grey scale.
7. Range control, adjusts the range over which the joystick will operate, and selects the mean aperture.
8. Readout of lens aperture.
9. Joystick, the main operational control, has three functions.
Twist to adjust master black level.
Forward/back to open/close iris.
Depress to switch channel to preview monitor.

63

Monitoring the Vision Signal

Two aspects of the vision signal which need constant monitoring are quality and quantity. Picture quality can be best assessed by reference to a correctly aligned colour monitor; again it cannot be stressed too much that the correct alignment of the colour monitor is of paramount importance for *consistently* good pictures. Many subjective assessments are made by reference to it.

The quantity or amplitude of the vision signal is best assessed by reference to an accurate waveform monitor (oscilloscope) which displays the picture information as a graph of continuously varying electrical signal which should be contained between the limits of black level and peak white.

A third aspect of the vision signal which needs checking is the colour information. Some features can be checked using a waveform monitor, but it is essential to use a special oscilloscope called a vectorscope when comparing two vision signals, e.g. for colour synchronisation or for checking the colour bar information (see pages 68 and 70). Usually, the test equipment is dual role and can be operated as either a waveform monitor or a vectorscope.

The TV waveform

The television waveform comprises two parts: above the base-line the picture signal; below it, the sync pulses. These two features are measured separately. Picture levels are assigned on a scale of IRE units from 0 to 100. Sync pulses are measured on a scale from 0 at the base-line (blanking level) down to −40 units.

The proportions of the waveform may instead be expressed in voltages. The picture occupies a maximum of 0.7 volt and the synchronising pulses 0.3 volt.

When monitoring a composite video signal, chrominance information looks like a high-frequency signal superimposed on the luminance waveform.

When monitoring a component signal, the luminance and colour difference signals are displayed side by side, sync pulses and coded chrominance information being absent.

Signal levels

Strictly speaking the only person to adjust the relative levels of the picture signal is the vision controller. These will be set by reference to a correctly aligned colour monitor and *occasional* reference to the waveform monitor.

It is therefore essential that the television system following the vision control operation has a 'unity gain', i.e. the vision signal remains an exact replica of the original signal at the vision control point. Hence the preoccupation with checking and setting the performance of vision signal paths/video-tape machines and line-up procedures, again using picture and waveform monitors to ensure that no picture distortion has taken place.

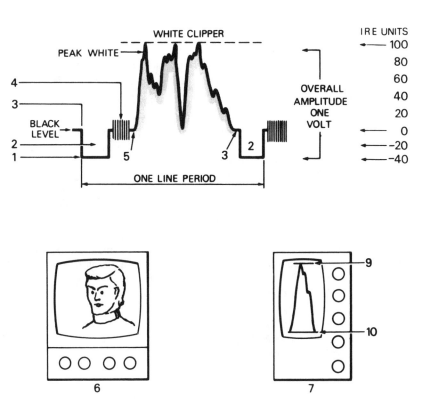

The video waveform

The video waveform includes picture information (coloured) together with
synchronising pulses. These are inserted in the line and field retrace (flyback) periods.
1. Synchronising level. 2. Line sync pulse, 3. Front porch. 4. Colour burst in back
porch. 5. Commencement of picture.

The television picture

The vision operator watches both his *picture monitor* (6) (for pictorial effect) and his
waveform monitor (7) (to ensure that the video waveform is within the system's
limits). The *waveform monitor* is an oscilloscope displaying the video waveform (at
line and field sweep-rates) against a calibrated graticule (IRE units), showing the
peak white level (9), and black level (10) limits (traced as reference lines on the
monitor tube).

Picture Monitors: Monochrome

A picture monitor is, to all appearances, a high-grade TV set without sound. It does not contain the circuitry for 'off air' reception, but is instead fed directly with a selected source's picture. It is the vital part in the control of camera pictures and represents the final link in the picture chain. The size of a monitor screen varies from a compact 5 in (125 mm) to 26 in (660 mm) (diagonal) for group viewing.

Monitor adjustment
An incorrectly adjusted picture monitor not only shows a misleading version of the camera's shot, but is liable to cause us to alter the staging, lighting, or picture quality inappropriately. A suit may look too dark, simply because our monitor is wrongly adjusted! Most monochrome monitors include a power switch, brightness, contrast, and picture scan controls (height and width). Switch on, and after a few minutes' warm-up time, check that the picture shape is right (4 by 3 aspect ratio). A test card containing a circular design reveals geometrical distortions.

Monitor line-up is easiest where we can display a suitable line-up chart or signal with a series of gradated tonal steps. Otherwise align all monitors to a static picture containing a full tonal range. First, turn the brightness and contrast controls fully down; then turn up the brightness control until a picture raster (the basic line-structure of the picture) is just seen. Now turn up the contrast control until a well-balanced full-tone picture with no defocusing in the highlights is seen.

Where a specially generated electronic monitor line-up signal is used, adjustments of brightness and contrast can be made in a few seconds. Alternatively, a standard grey scale step wedge can be used.

All high-grade picture monitors are fitted with a black-level clamp (fixed black level) to ensure that tonal values remain constant, regardless of changes of picture content.

Monitor termination
To avoid distortions and loss of signal strength, a picture monitor is provided with circuitry (a 75 ohm termination) that matches it to its video source. Where more than one monitor is to be supplied from the same source, only one termination is required.

Monitor suitability
While some monitors reproduce the pictures from helical-scan videotape recorders quite satisfactorily, others do not. Instead, the picture is unstable, and accompanied by jitter and synchronising problems. It is as well, therefore, when selecting monitors for such a system, to ensure that they will reproduce helical VTR signals effectively.

Check that the colour temperature of the display phosphor is suitable for the application required. Most domestic monochrome monitors have a very blue phosphor and are unsuitable for use alongside colour monitors (correlated colour temperature 6500 K).

66

Monitor line-up signal

A multi-tone, electronically generated signal enables us to iine-up picture monitors to a consistent standard. The signal from this picture line-up generating equipment (PLUGE) is as shown.

1. Line sync pulse.
2. Peak white signal (100%).
3. Overall background (0%).
4. Background tone (+3%).
5. Background (−3%).
6. Mid grey.

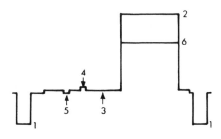

Adjusting the monitor

The monitor *contrast* control is adjusted for the required highlight level (e.g. 25 foot-lamberts). Adjust the *brightness* control so that the black bar appears black, and the dark grey bar can only just be distinguished.

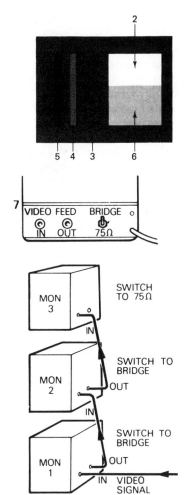

Monitor bridging

When a picture signal is to be looped through a series of monitors, only the last in the chain should be *terminated* (i.e. a resistance switched across its video input). A switch at the rear of a picture monitor will be marked BRIDGE (or HIGH and 75Ω. This should be positioned as in the diagram.

67

Picture Monitors: Colour

With the advent of micro-electronics and the inherent stability of such devices the cost of colour monitors has been reduced to the point where they are as cheap as good monochrome monitors. Servicing of colour is more complicated than for monochrome monitors, therefore it is advisable not to install too many colour monitors in a studio control room.

Generally, monochrome monitors will be used when permanently displaying a particular vision source, i.e. Cam1, Cam2, videotape etc. Colour monitors will usually be switched to particular sources as necessary. Lighting and vision control will require, in addition to the transmission monitor, at least two assignable colour monitors.

Each monitor should be able to display composite, component or separate Red, Green and Blue signal sources.

Monitor grades
Colour monitors generally fall into one of two categories, Grade 1 and Grade 2. Grade 1 monitors are of the highest quality and are used in areas where critical assessment of picture quality is required. They have a good specification on stability, picture geometry, colour rendition, convergence, picture sharpness, stabilised black level and ability to operate in simple PAL mode (PAL system only), and naturally are expensive.

Grade 2 monitors have a less demanding specification than Grade 1 and are consequently cheaper. However, they still need to be very stable in operation and perform far better than a normal domestic television set.

Colour monitor line-up
The importance of good, consistent colour monitor line-up cannot be stressed enough. The colour monitor is the focus for all subjective colour judgements and technical assessment of picture quality. Its alignment should therefore be considered to be one of the most important tasks, especially in the lighting and vision control area.

Monitor line-up test signals
Colour monitor line-ups should be checked regularly. Several test signals are required, namely:
● *PLUGE signal*—to set brightness and contrast in a similar way to monochrome monitors.
● *Grille signal*—to check accuracy of the convergence of the scanning electron beams in the display tube.
● Neutral step wedge—to check the grey scale of the monitor to ensure no colour casts on neutral tones from black to white and to set the white point of the display (6500 K).
● *Colour bars*—to check saturation of the colour display.

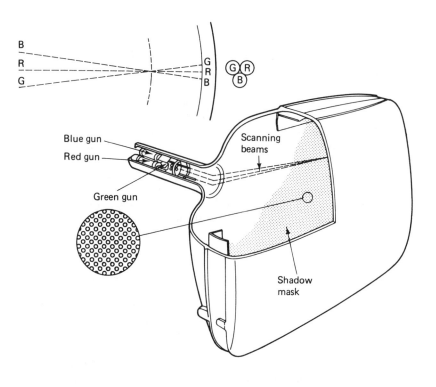

Colour monitors: the shadow-mask tube

Although other types of display tube are available, notably the slot mask, the shadow-mask tube is most suitable in a studio where the optimum performance is required. The electrons from the gun controlled by the red signal are arranged to strike the screen only where there is a red phosphor dot. The beams from the blue and green guns likewise only strike the blue and green phosphor dots. The shadow mask allows the beams to strike only their associated phosphor dots.

The screen has almost one million dots, one-third for each colour. The naked eye cannot resolve the dots at normal viewing distances and the eye integrates the mixture according to the relative excitation of the three phosphors.

Although one set of scanning coils is used, additional magnets and coils are used to ensure the beams scan correctly over the whole mesh. The grille test pattern (described opposite) enables the necessary adjustments to be made. A grey-scale chart enables adjustment of the relative excitation of the phosphors (the 'gain' and 'background' of each amplifier) to be correct over the whole tonal range.

Synchronisation

The television picture is scanned systematically in a series of parallel lines. Each picture is actually covered in two successive scanning patterns (odd and even fields), which are automatically interlaced to form a fully scanned picture (frame).

The television pick-up device generates the picture information on a line-by-line basis. At the end of each line, the scanning spot flies back to begin the next. This continues until a complete field has been scanned, when the scanning spot returns quickly to the top of the picture to commence the next field. To ensure that this scanning process is carried out with precision, and the entire TV system is synchronised from camera to receiver, special 'sync' pulses are generated to initiate the line and fields scanning actions. A special *synchronising pulse generator* (SPG) produces these pulses, which are then added to the picture information. Any studio with more than one camera needs an SPG to act as the common reference point for all picture and synchronisable sound sources. The SPG is the heart of the studio system— failure of this one device causes total failure of the whole system. A back-up spare is therefore essential. Many pieces of studio equipment have their own self-contained SPGs.

Picture timing

In television, we are dealing with signals that change in less than a millionth of a second. So, when a series of video signals travel over any appreciable distance by cables of different path lengths, we find that their arrival times at a given point are dissimilar. Consequently, their synchronising pulses appear time-displaced. To avoid this dilemma, all cable lengths to a vision mixing point should normally be identical, whether from cameras, telecine, slide scanners, videotape, etc. (all are made equal to the longest). Without accurate picture timing, sideways displacement or definition loss may occur on mixes, while in colour systems a hue change could arise.

External picture sources

A problem exists when two vision sources use different SPGs. They must be made synchronous, i.e. in step with each other, before mixing, chroma key etc. are possible. This may be achieved by using *genlock*, a process whereby one of the SPGs is controlled (slaved) by the vision signal derived from the second source. Most lightweight cameras have a genlock facility.

An alternative solution is to use a synchroniser. This is a digital device which stores a complete picture, reading out the stored information in step with the local syncs (local SPG), effectively rescanning the picture in synchronism with the locally generated pictures.

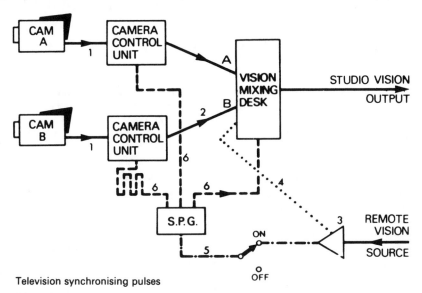

Television synchronising pulses

Monochrome

Line drive (LD)	Synchronises line-scanning process (at the end of each scanned line).
Field drive (FD)	Establishes field synchronisation. (Scanning beam returns to top of raster on completion of each field.)
Mixed blanking (MB)	Picture information is suppressed by blanking pulses, to permit insertion of line and field sync pulses.
Mixed syncs (MS)	A composite sync signal consisting of both line and field sync pulses. Required by monitors/receivers to maintain horizontal sweep synchronism during field retrace period.

Colour—additional signals required

Colour subcarrier (SC)	A constant frequency generated as a reference for colour information. (Added to the luminance signal to form an encoded signal for transmission.)
Reference burst	A short burst of subcarrier frequency inserted into the back porch of line sync pulse (i.e. once per line), to ensure correct reproduced hue.
Pal Ident	A reference signal to identify the phase of the colour burst, which alternates on successive lines.

Synchronising the camera system
The synchronising pulse generator (SPG) ensures that all the video sources are in exact synchronism. This avoids such problems as picture cut-off, roll-over, tearing, displacement, that would otherwise arise. Where remote picture sources are used (e.g. outside broadcast unit, remotes) their system must be synchronous with the studio if pictures are to be mixed or superimposed. In one system (genlock) sync pulses are derived from the remote source to drive the receiving studio's pulse train. In a simple set-up one camera (with built-in SPG) may be used to genlock another, thus avoiding the use of a separate SPG.

1. Camera cables. 2. Video output connections. 3. Video distribution amplifier. 4. Video feed ('remote' to mixing desk). 5. Genlock input. 6. Synchronising cables (note that all must be the same length).

71

Vision Signal Distribution

Once one of the available picture sources in the studio has been selected by the switcher in the production control room, this picture needs to be distributed—to various monitor points in the building, to recording systems, to central routing areas (e.g. continuity, network control, etc.).

Distribution amplifier
This is a special amplifier which usually has no gain. It provides many identical separate output signals all electrically isolated from each other. The output is an exact copy of the input signal.

Termination panel
As outlined above, the studio-output picture signal must be distributed to a variety of areas: videotape, telecine, lecture halls, viewing rooms, etc. This is achieved by a patching panel in the studio apparatus area, enabling picture (and sound) signals to be routed to selected points.

Cable distribution
Picture sources can be fed to monitors or videotape recorders only over relatively short lengths of video cable (up to 200 metres/yards). Long cable runs produce degradation of pictures (especially colour signals) unless special equalisation amplifiers are used en route.

Radio frequency distribution
If many monitors located at remote points from the studio centre are to be fed, a system of RF (radio frequency) distribution can be used. The picture to be distributed is fed to a modulator unit, which converts the video to a radio signal. This is then routed by coaxial cable to its destination. The picture is viewed at the receiving point on a conventional television receiver. RF distribution has the main advantage that many pictures can be channelled at different frequencies along the same cable.

Microwave links
It may be easier to install a microwave television link between two buildings if a permanent vision circuit is needed over a distance of more than one mile. In many countries prior permission of the Telecommunication Authority must be obtained for external picture distribution.

Fibre optic links
It may be necessary to distribute several television pictures simultaneously over reasonably long distance, between remote studio sites. As an alternative to conventional cable circuits, fibre optic links offer a cheaper method. Many individual circuits can be contained within one fibre link. Sophisticated sending and receiving equipment is needed, but greater reliability and immunity to interference is offered by these links than is normal with conventional copper cables.

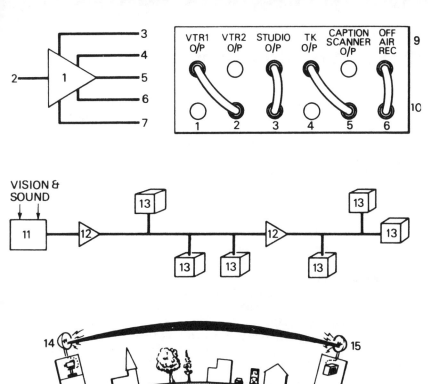

The distribution amplifier
The distribution amplifier (1) has zero gain and provides identical video signals at a series of isolated outputs (e.g. 3–5 points). Video input (2) can be distributed to several outputs (3–7), e.g. to transmission monitor; floor monitor; technical director; engineering check monitor.

The termination panel
The termination panel (8) facilitates distribution of picture sources to their various destinations. Available sources are located at the top of the patch panel (9). Potential destinations (1–6) are arranged in the bottom row (10). Flexible coaxial cables or rigid U-links route the video.

Radio frequency distribution
For larger installations, the picture and sound may be fed into a *modulator* (11). The resultant modulated radio frequency carrier is distributed by coaxial cable. Distribution amplifiers (12) may be required en route to boost the signal. Television receivers are used as monitors (13).

Microwave links
Here the modulated signal is transmitted from a high point, via a parabolic microwave aerial (14). At the receiving point (15) (which must be within sight of the transmitter) the signal is demodulated (detected) and the original video and audio signals recovered.

73

Production Control Room

This area is the heart of any television complex. It is here that the production is controlled, and the operations directed. In this room programme and technical staff watch a series of preview monitors and the output of the vision mixing desk, which appears on the 'transmission' monitor. This is the studio output, which now passes to the distribution system for recording or transmission. The programme sound is heard over a nearby loudspeaker. Desk 'talkback microphones' pass instruction and guidance to the studio crew.

The ideal layout is still a matter of debate; in some studio centres all technical and programme staff operate in one area. Other arrangements utilise three separate rooms for vision, sound and production control.

Picture monitors
The main features of the production control room is its bank of picture monitors previewing all picture sources contributing to the programme. Most show continuously the output of their channel (e.g. Camera 1), certain others are switched as required. The transmission monitor is centrally mounted above the preview monitors. Picture monitor layout should be just below the horizontal eyeline. The viewing distance is ideally six to eight times the viewing diagonal of the monitor screen. Nearer than that, it is tiring to continually scan around; more distant, and we lose detail.

Environment
Two levels of room lighting should be available: normal overall illumination, and localised operational lighting. The operational lighting must be arranged so that sufficient light is available to read programme scripts, floor plans, etc., with ease, and to quickly locate and operate technical equipment; extraneous light should not spill on to preview monitors. The control room should be carpeted to improve acoustics, and have effective ventilation.

Layout
Control positions for all production and technical personnel are arranged along a laminated-plastic desk (around 70 cm high), housing such facilities as the vision mixing panel, talkback systems, remote operational controls for cameras, lighting dimmers and remote control of VTR and telecine machines.

Care spent in the design of the production desk layout will reap benefits in future productions.

Remember that additional production staff (e.g. producer, designer, wardrobe and make-up staff) *may* require access and seating; but don't allow the control room (gallery) to be an area where people can drift in and out at will during rehearsals.

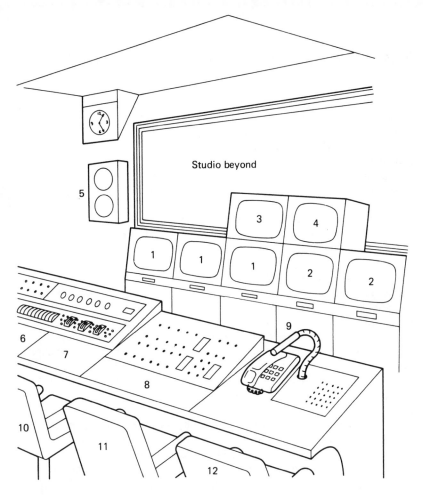

Production control room

In this typical small studio set-up we see the main operational positions overlooking the preview monitors, 1–4.
1. Cameras 1–3 preview monitors, left to right (monochrome).
2. Additional preview monitors for videotape etc.
3. Transmission monitor (colour).
4. Colour preview monitor.
5. Loudspeaker.
6. Lighting controls.
7. Operational camera controls.
8. Vision mixer (switcher) control panel.
9. Talkback microphone.
10. Lighting (technical) director.
11. Vision mixer (switcher).
12. Director.
Where space is limited the sound mixer might also be housed here.

Typical viewing conditions

Seating should not be positioned too close or too far from the picture monitors; six to eight times the picture diagonal is preferable. Shielded overhead lighting illuminates desk controls and scripts without spilling on to monitor screens in the darkened room.

Vision Mixer or Switcher: Function

The vision mixer or switcher is the destination point for all picture sources in the studio. The output of all the studio cameras, telecine machines, videotape recorders (when 'playing in' inserts to a programme), caption scanners (film strips and slides) are connected to the inputs of the vision mixing unit (or switcher).

The function of the desk is to edit together (by cutting, mixing, etc.) all these various contributions to the production, as the director has planned.

The output of the switcher (studio output) is connected, via distribution amplifiers, to the transmission monitor in the production control area, and to the transmission chain, check monitors, etc., that comprise the television complex. The switcher is located in the production control area.

Vision mixer design

Although many designs of switcher exist, each with its own merits and limitations, the principles involved are simple enough. A flexible vision mixer should be able to cut, mix, fade up or out, superimpose, and provide effects facilities such as wipes, split screen, chroma key and downstream keyer.

The operational panel of the switcher should be well laid out and easy to operate. Figure 1 opposite shows a typical panel layout for a basic switcher in which each picture source is available for button selection on a number of horizontal 'busbars'. This switcher incorporates all the facilities mentioned above plus a master fader.

The downstream keyer provides the facility for black/white captions to be inserted after all the switching functions, thus ensuring that a caption is 'in front' of all parts of the picture. The captions, although faded up, are not superimposed but inserted into the picture, i.e. inlaid, for better legibility.

The master fader enables the output of the switcher to be easily faded to black/faded up from black.

What to look for

No matter how inexpensive your system your vision mixer should fit your projected requirements. All switching operations should be accomplished without any 'break up' or 'roll' on the transmission monitor. Also the quality of the outgoing picture should be identical to that of the input picture.

Be warned! Sophisticated mixing panels do not in themselves produce better production techniques. Unskilled operation can lead to embarrassing 'on air' errors. Even when mistakes can be rectified by re-recording, this can prove time-consuming—and is often costly.

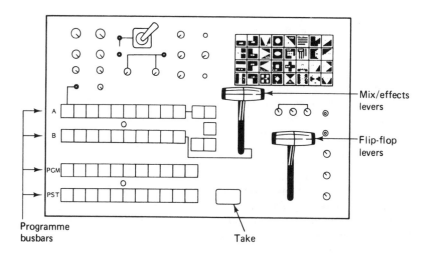

Programme
busbars

Take

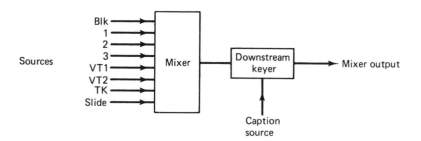

Sources

Typical panel for a small studio vision mixer

Each picture source (channel) is connected to the same numbered button on each of
the busbars or banks of the mixer (A, B, Programme, Preset). The first button is fed
with Black; usually this is followed by Camera 1, Camera 2, Camera 3 etc.
This mixer will allow cutting between sources on the programme busbar, mixing
between two sources by presetting the new source on the preset busbar and
changing the faders (bottom left). Complex wipes and chroma key set-ups are
achieved using the A/B banks together with the wipe selection panel, chroma-key
controls and the mix/effects levers.
A useful addition to this is a downstream keyer which inserts captions into the final
picture compilation (2). This enables captions to be faded up/down, and also allows
the captions to have black edges/drop shadow/colour borders to improve the visibility
of the lettering and allow the colour of the captions to be changed to suit the
programme material.

Vision Mixer: General Facilities

The sophisticated switcher offers all the visual effects (and more!) to the TV director that are available in the film-making process. Effects that require time, skill, and costly auxiliary equipment in film, can be achieved in TV at the touch of a button.

The cut
Even the simplest mixer can cut between picture sources. The cut is an instantaneous switch from one picture to another. As with all types of transition, there must be no frame-roll or flash evident on the picture at the moment of cutting.

The mix or dissolve
Here the transition is less pronounced. As the faders are operated the established picture (e.g. Camera 2) fades away, while the new picture (e.g. telecine) progressively appears. Both picture sources appear on the screen simultaneously. Obviously the speed of the mix is dictated by the production requirement. A mix can take several seconds or can be almost instantaneous.

The fade-up/fade-out
As the fader is operated a picture can be made to either appear from or disappear into a black screen. Two ways of achieving this effect are common: (1) a mix or dissolve from a picture to black level set up on the normal mix/effects panel of the mixer; (2) if a master fader is incorporated at the output of the mixer, operating this fader produces a dissolve from or to black.

The superimposition
By fading up two or more picture sources together, we obtain a superimposition. This device may be used to add titling to an existing picture, or special montage effects.

Preview facilities
Certain mixers have a separate preview bank (preview bus), with the video output connected to an associated monitor. This enables us to check any selected non-studio picture source (e.g. a remote) before switching it to the transmission channel. It assists, too, in preparing a combination picture (of two or more cameras' shots).

As it is operated, the vision mixing desk also switches corresponding cue lights (tally lights) on the cameras to denote which is 'on air' (for camera operators, floor manager, artistes, etc.).

Practice varies as to who operates the vision mixing desk. It may be a specialist operator (the switcher or vision mixer) or the technical director; in small studios and in outside broadcast units the director may operate the vision mixing panel.

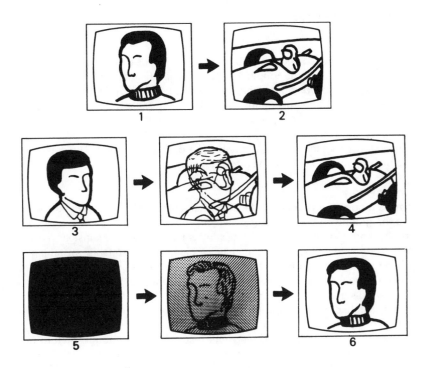

The cut
An instantaneous change, achieved by pressing the cut-button of the second channel.
e.g. *From* Cam 1 (1) *To* Telecine (2).
The *cut* is used when action in the two scenes is consecutive.

The mix
The first picture (3) fades in intensity, the second simultaneously strengthening to full intensity (4). (Holding the controls midway produces *superimpositions*.) Achieved by fading between the banks, different sources having been selected on their respective banks (e.g. Cam 2 on Bank A to Telecine on Bank B). The *mix* usually signifies a lapse of time.

Fade up
The screen is black (5), the picture gradually strengthens to full intensity (6). The required channel is selected on one bank, but the associated half of the dual fader is faded out (split fader). As the fader is operated, the picture appears. Moving the control to 'out', the picture fades away.

Vision Mixer: Special Effects

The use of special effects facilities on switchers can improve the scope of production capabilities.

The wipe
Available on most switchers, this can best be described as one picture gradually replacing the original picture. The direction of entry can be horizontal, vertical, diagonal, circular, diamond shaped and so on. The 'edge' of the wipe can be sharply defined (hard) or electronically defocused (soft).

The split screen
This is a wipe which is frozen at some pre-determined point. The composite picture is made up from two picture sources.

Chroma key
This is a powerful production facility whereby part of one picture, known as the foreground source, is electronically inserted in another picture, known as the background source. The foreground subject is shot against an area of plain saturated colour backing, usually blue, and a suitable switching or keying signal, derived from the foreground camera, is used to operate a fast switch. When the foreground camera sees blue only, i.e. the blue background, the keying signal will be at a maximum; this results in the background source being switched to the output of the switcher.

Obviously the foreground subject must not contain any of the keying colour, otherwise spurious keying will result. The background picture may contain all colours since it is not involved in generating the keying signal. Good results with chroma key require careful planning and lighting.

Caption key
This facility enables white lettering, from black/white captions or an electronic caption generator, to be inserted into a picture, resulting in much greater clarity than using a superimposition.

Black edger or borderline generator
Even the use of caption key will not help the visibility of captions if they are inserted against a white or similar high luminance background. A black-edger puts a black edge around lettering to make it stand out. On some switchers the thickness can be independently varied on the horizontal and vertical strokes, producing a 'drop-shadow' three-dimensional effect, and the edge may be selected to be any colour (hue, saturation and luminance).

Colour synthesiser
A colour synthesiser is able to produce coloured pictures from black and white graphics. Both the background and the letters can be selected to any hue, saturation and luminance.

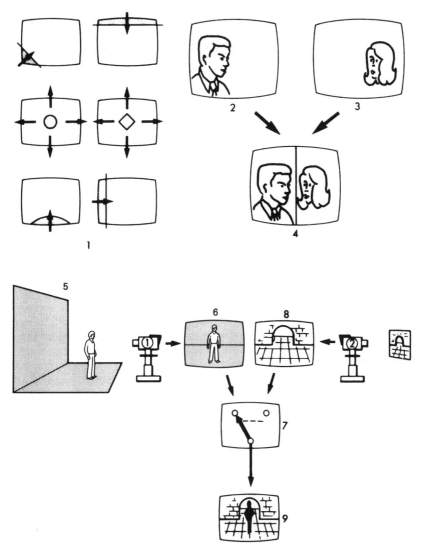

Wipes

Speed of wipe is set by rate at which wipe fader is moved on effects unit. All wipe pattern directions can be reversed. Typical patterns are shown here (1).

Split screen

By stopping a wipe pattern at an intermediate position, we achieve a screen that is bisected (split-screen) or an inserted area.

Here the picture from two sources (2 & 3) have been combined in a split-screen (4) using a horizontal wipe.

Chroma key

The subject stands before a blue backing (5). Its camera output (Camera 1) (6) is fed to the chroma key switch (7). Whenever blue appears in this shot, the switch operates and presents the background scene on Camera 2, instead (8). The combined composite shot shows the subject within the background scene (9). Note that the floor needs to be blue for long shots.

Other Analogue Vision Facilities

Most of the following are not essential for the basic studio, but depending on the style of programmes and level of sophistication required they can significantly enhance programme presentation.

Floor monitors
At least one studio floor monitor, pluggable or switchable to any source, as well as studio output for presenters, floor managers etc., is essential. Often, presenters need to see incoming videotape to pace their introduction.

Projection systems
Pictures may be combined electronically using vision mixer special effects facilities or by using digital video effect devices. These have replaced studio-based projection equipment. However, video systems using high-intensity projectors and high-reflectivity screens can produce acceptable images under normal studio lighting conditions and are useful to display previously recorded or current images to a larger audience than would normally be possible by using conventional picture monitors.

Slide scanners
35mm photographs may be required for a particular production. These are normally held in an electronic picture store and can be recalled at random and presented as a normal video source on the vision mixer. These stored images are originated from a slide scanner which could be a dedicated machine or part of a telecine machine, and comes in a variety of standards from cheap camera system to sophisticated flying spot version with digital colour correction controls.

Caption projection unit
A cheap method of presenting slides on a programme is the caption projection unit (CPU), which consists of one or two projectors and a screen housed in a cabinet to shield the screen from extraneous light. Any studio camera can be pointed at the screen and used to frame the shot as required. The quality of images produced by this system is relatively poor although it does allow selective framing of the original photograph. If two projectors are used with a dissolve unit, then mixes between images are possible using one unit and one camera.

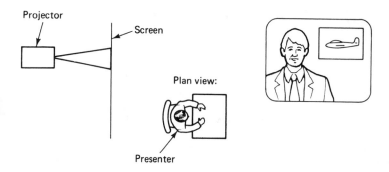

Large screen projector
A typical presenter situation with an over-shoulder picture from a large screen projector.

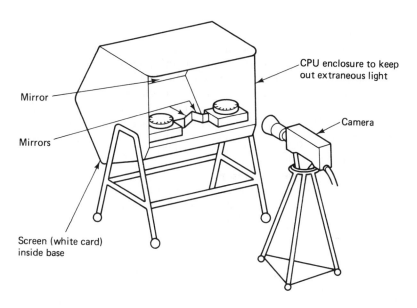

Caption projection unit
The CPU is a simple, home-made device for presenting slides by pointing a camera at a projected image. The picture can be framed at will and slides mixed using a dissolve unit (not shown). The picture quality is inferior to a slide scanner.

Digital Video Technology

Digital technology offers significant advances in quality, delivers effects not possible with traditional analogue equipment and speeds up the achievement of a polished product. It has revolutionised graphics and although costs are high for small installations, it is becoming more attractive with the falling price of computer memory. It is now possible to build an almost entirely digital station that is not prohibitively more expensive than a traditional installation, however, top-end devices remain expensive and the cost-conscious user needs to consider carefully the level at which to invest. Hiring a facility, if it is only occasionally needed, may be a cost-effective alternative.

Whilst some advantages of digital technology may be marginal for the small facility, it seems likely that the availability of traditional analogue equipment will reduce in the future but not in the short term. The decision, therefore, is not an easy one. The major advances afforded by digital technology are most sharply focused on video effects, graphics and post-production.

Digital graphics are discussed on page 88. Digital post-production is a more recent development which has been made possible by the enormous increase in computer memory now available. This enables random access of recorded material and thus speeds up the editing process considerably. For a more comprehensive discussion see pages 164 and 166.

Digital video effects
There are many types of digital video effects (DVE). Basic devices can manipulate one picture in two dimensions and offer a freeze frame capability. Sophisticated machines permit the manipulation of two or more pictures simultaneously, can introduce perspective into a two-dimensional image and apply distortions that bend, zoom, rotate on any axis, do page turns etc., as well as memorise sequences. In general, the more sophisticated the device the more it costs.

Picture stores
Often installed in the graphics area, picture stores are able to record stills or 'grab' moving pictures and automatically index them. Browsing through the stores by displaying a 'polyphoto' is possible and picture selection is fast. Some advanced equipments offer the full archiving facilities of a picture library.

Standards conversion
The British television standard uses 625 lines to each picture, with a picture repetition rate of 25 per second. The American standard has 525 lines and 30 pictures per second. Three main colour systems are in use: NTSC (mainly USA and Japan), SECAM (Francophone countries and a modified version in Eastern Europe) and PAL (most other parts of the world including UK). Programmes cannot be interchanged without conversion. Standards converters are usually hired when required, although domestic quality VHS recorders are now available for viewing quality conversions. Some videotape machines and monitors have a multi-standard playback facility.

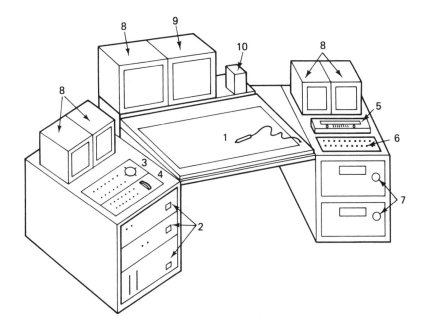

Typical digital work station

Although the above devices may be independently fed to the studio they may also work in combinations or off-line to generate programme material prior to a studio session or afterwards to 'doctor' pre-recorded material.

1. Pallette and stylus for computer graphics machine.
2. Electronics associated with the various devices.
3. Digital video effects (DVE) control panel.
4. Vision mixer/downstream keyer.
5. Edit control panel for videotape machines.
6. Character generator.
7. Videotape machines.
8. Preview monitors.
9. Output/transmission monitor.
10. Loudspeaker (another may be required for studio talkback if on-line use is anticipated).

Other devices such as slide-file and colour correctors may also be made available to the work station.

85

Television Prompters

Prompting during a television production may be necessary to aid recall of forgotten lines, as an *aide-mémoire* in the form of a list of subjects to be covered, or the complete text (unlearned) to be read to camera as if delivered spontaneously.

Prompt card
The *aide-mémoire* type of prompting is often met in current affairs or educational productions. In its simplest form it may be a large card held up by the floor manager as near to the presenter's eye-line as possible (when he/she is not on camera).

Hearing aid
A more sophisticated communications aid is the unobtrusive hearing aid worn by the presenter and connected to the director's microphone by a switch. The director operates the switch when he wishes to pass cues, up-to-date information etc. to assist the speaker, unheard by the microphone or others in the studio. Known as switched talkback, it should naturally be used sparingly and considerately and never whilst the presenter is speaking or about to speak.

Electronic prompter
A type of prompter that contains the complete production text takes several forms. A system still occasionally found is the mechanically driven paper roll. The script is typed at a base station onto a cash-register roll of paper. This roll is viewed by a small industrial camera, its televised image appearing on the prompter picture monitor with reversed scans. This is viewed by the speaker through a semi-reflecting mirror in front of the camera lens. It now appears that the speaker is addressing the viewer directly. If necessary, film or videotape may also be displayed on the prompter monitor with the script superimposed. The eye movements of the speaker are hardly detectable as he reads the script. Last minute alterations are possible by simply cutting out redundant passages with scissors and joining on additions with clear adhesive tape, or for small changes, sticking a blank piece of paper over the script and writing in the alterations. Speed is controlled by an operator or the presenter. A more advanced system now universally replacing the paper roll couples the monitor to a special word processor. The operator can delete, add or alter the text, the word processor automatically justifying as the changes are made. The equipment is ideally suited to prepared statements, speeches and news situations where changes are often made whilst the programme is on air. Speed control is again by an operator or the presenter and most can link into other computer networks, e.g. news systems for automatic downloading of scripts.

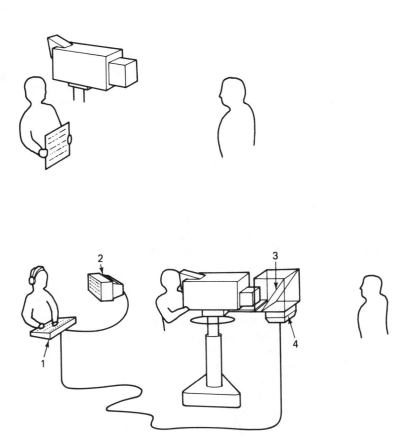

Digital prompter
The elements of a digital prompter include a specially programmed word processor (1), a monitor for the operator (2), and a hood attached to the front of the camera containing a semi-reflecting mirror (3) which enables the presenter to look straight at the lens when reading his script displayed on the reverse scanned monitor (4) fitted beneath the hood. The operator remains in contact with the director through headphones.

87

Graphics

Graphics are integral to any programme and range from a simple caption made from cardboard and rub-on lettering, now eliminated from all but the most basic of facilities, to highly sophisticated electronic creations.

The well-designed graphic adds to the style and professional presentation of a programme and to the viewer's understanding and appreciation thereof. Not only do graphics encompass highly creative artwork, they are essential for the presentation of data or statistics which can otherwise be difficult to interpret.

Correct aspect ratio
The width : height ratio of the television screen is known as the aspect ratio. This is currently 4:3, although there are plans to move to 16:9 in the future. Non-original work such as photographs may be any shape and a decision may have to be made to frame only part of the picture or have a border showing on screen. Many TV screens also cut off the edges of pictures and it is therefore wise to compose graphics leaving about a 5% margin around the edges. The area inside this notional border is known as the 'safe' area.

Character generators
Titles and credits are almost always created electronically using a character generator, namely a computer that enables characters to be typed directly onto a television screen and memorised for later use. Dedicated keys can select different character styles and fonts as well as colours for foregrounds and backgrounds. Most have the facility to roll or crawl captions at variable speeds and some can even import logos, frame grab moving pictures and even manipulate pictures like a limited DVE (see page 84).

Whilst coloured foregrounds and backgrounds are sometimes useful, white on black is most commonly used as the graphics are usually overlaid onto a background picture and white provides greatest clarity (see page 80).

Artwork
Original artwork is seldom done on paper these days. Painting devices using an electronic tablet and a pressure-sensitive pen are the almost universal method used in the industry. A range of equipment is available to suit different pockets. Top-end equipment provides different drawing effects and thicknesses such as pen, brush, chalk etc. Standard shapes are easily generated as is filling, shading, cutting and pasting or rotating parts of the design. A comprehensive palatte of colours is available some allowing almost infinite mixing possibilities. Some machines are up-gradable: starting with a simple painting device, one can add new features when the funds are available. At the top-end animation and editing are also possible.

The small user would be wise to consider investing appropriately to meet regular needs and hiring-in as necessary from a dedicated facilities house.

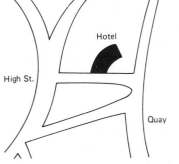

Readability
Do not use lettering that is too small
to be read comfortably.

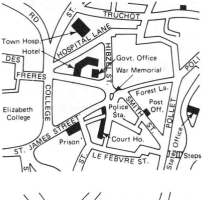

Muddled
An example of an attempt to use a
real map for an illustration. The
result is too confusing for the
viewer to assimilate.

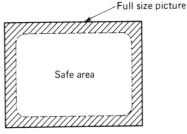

Stylising
A stylised map showing the main
features, which is much more
readable on the television screen. A
flat-bed photographic copy stand
fitted with a video camera can be
useful for stills, maps etc., to be
'grabbed' and modified by the
graphics artist.

Avoid
Wrinkles in captions.
Small writing.
Glossy surfaces.
Acetate gels over illustrations.
Lettering outside 'safe' area.

Approx. 10% margin all round

89

Lighting: Overall System

Any TV lighting system has to provide the correct quantity of light on the subject (illumination) and, for colour television, must also provide light of the correct quality (colour temperature). To satisfy these needs it requires light fittings (luminaires), means of supporting them and a system for controlling the light output from each lamp.

How elaborate our facilities need to be will be influenced by:
● Camera sensitivity.
● Size of acting area.
● Height of lighting ceiling (lighting grid).
● Turnround time required between programmes.

If the initial design is for a simple lighting suspension but more flexible arrangements are likely to be needed at a later date, the ceiling and steelwork to meet the later requirements should, if possible, be put in at the time of building the studio. It is difficult and expensive to add these features later.

Camera sensitivity
The sensitivity of the camera channel determines the lighting level required: the subject illumination. It is usually quoted for a given signal/noise ratio in terms of subject illumination when operating the camera at a normal lens aperture. It should be noted that the use of any front-of-lens prompting device will need an increase in the required lighting level.

Size of acting area
In the small TV studio the whole of the available staging area is gradually used and our lighting set-up needs to accommodate several adjoining regions. The precise nature of the action in each changes for each programme and the lighting system must be flexible enough to cater for these different situations. If initially, for economy reasons, only part of the studio is being used, the lighting system can be restricted accordingly. This will cut costs but will make the system less adaptable.

Height of studio grid
The height of the studio has been discussed earlier (page 20). The maximum height of the luminaires above the studio floor is directly related to this and so also is the maximum lamp throw (lamp-to-subject distance). This factor coupled with camera sensitivity fixes the wattage of luminaires to be used.

Turnround time
How long it takes to modify a lighting set-up to suit a new production is largely determined by the suspension system, and is discussed on pages 92/94. Generally, the more flexible systems offer the quickest turnround.

Studio lighting levels (1 lumen/m² = 1 lux)	*Power requirements (based on the total studio floor area)*
500–800 lumens/m²	250 watts/m²
Add extra power to cater for cyclorama lighting	

Colour camera type	*Typical studio lighting requirement*	**Nominal lens aperture*
3 x 1 lead oxide vidicons	approx. 800 lux	f/2.8
3 x ⅔" lead oxide vidicons	600-750 lux	f/2.0
3 x ⅔" format CCD	200-500 lux	f/2.0
3 x ½" format CCD	approx. 300 lux	f/1.4

* For a given shot this lens aperture will maintain similar depths of field for the different format sizes.
† This will be close to the maximum lens aperture, so it may be more convenient to operate at f/2.0. This will enable the lens iris to be 'opened-up' as well as 'stopped-down' during vision control operations. Depth of field will increase, and sensitivity will halve, as a consequence.

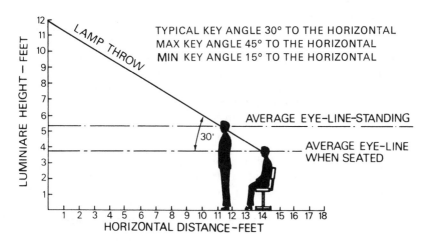

Studio lighting requirements

Simple Lighting Supports

The lighting suspension system provides the means for positioning the luminaires in the studio. It should:

● Be of sufficient height to enable the correct lamp throw and vertical lighting angle to be achieved. (We must avoid steep or overhead lighting.)

● Allow the lighting director to position luminaires to within 0.6 m (2 ft) of any point in the studio.

● Be easy to move luminaires around the suspension system.

Floor stands
Luminaires mounted on extendable floor stands are useful for static situations but have many disadvantages. They are generally limited in height to about two metres and can obstruct cameras, boom and artistes. They are liable to be knocked, disturbing the setting of the luminaire and perhaps even causing it to fall over. Placed upstage (i.e. in distant areas of the scene) a stand-mounted luminaire has to be hidden to avoid its appearing in shot.

Despite these criticisms, however, a selecion of floor stands can prove very useful for lighting through scenic openings (windows), and where we need to add an extra luminaire quickly.

Luminaires on flats
There are various fixtures available for mounting luminaires on flats. These have two main limitations. Heavy lamps cannot be used (the scenery would probably fall over!) and, obviously, lamps can be attached only where suitably constructed scenery exists.

Telescopic tubes
This is a very flexible system but has the disadvantage that it can be used only for lightweight luminaires and where studio construction permits. It consists of concentric telescopic tubes which have large rubber pads on both ends. To use, one end of the pole, which is spring loaded, is compressed, and the pole length adjusted to the ceiling height. The spring-loaded section is then released. This jams the pole firmly between the floor and the ceiling. Luminaires can be attached to the pole, or, by using an additional vertical pole, a cross member can be fitted, to enable further lamps to be included.

Lightweight track
This system is useful for studios of limited height (up to 3 m, 10 ft). The luminaires use a special mounting which enables them to be slid along a power track fastened to the ceiling. By dividing the ceiling up with a number of separately powered tracks, good coverage of the studio can be obtained. The limitation of this system is the weight restriction on the light fittings used.

Lightweight stands

The lightweight stand (1) should only be used with lightweight luminaires. The 'turtle' (2) is used when a luminaire is to be floor mounted. Short stands (3) are also useful, as is a clamp arm which can be fitted to normal stands to enable a luminaire to be mounted lower than 1 m (3 ft). Wind-up stands (4) are also used for heavy luminaires.

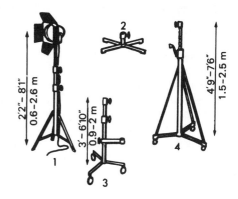

Scenic clamps

Lightweight lamps can be inserted into clamps attached to scenic flats. Here are two types, one to mount on the top of the flat (5), the other with a drop-arm to lower the height of the luminaire (6).

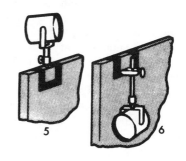

Lightweight telescopic tubes

Spring-loaded telecopic tubes (7) wedge between ceiling and floor, to support lightweight lamps. Auxiliary cross-tubes (8) can be introduced. The system provides considerable flexibility for confined spaces.

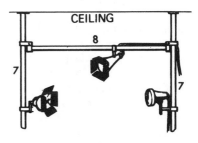

Lightweight ceiling track

Lightweight ceiling track—easy to install. Currently tracks are available which have 1, 2 and 4 separate circuits. On the multi-circuit track, connection is made to the appropriate circuit by means of sliding contacts (9).

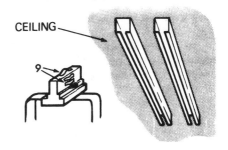

93

Lighting Suspension Systems

A flexible lighting suspension system is one which allows for easy and rapid positioning of a luminaire to within 0.6 m (2 ft) of any position in the studio. This enables a short turnround time to be achieved and allows the lighting director to position his lamps in a reasonably precise way. Flexibility usually requires an expensive suspension system. The most elaborate facilities (lighting bars on motorised hoists, and motorised telescopic methods) are not included here, as their high cost is not usually justified for the small television studio.

Pipe grid
This system has the advantages of being relatively cheap, and easy to modify. All the piping and clamps are standard construction items. The grid consists of a horizontal framework made from tubular piping of 48 mm diameter. The spacing between the grid members should ideally be 1.2 m (4 ft). The height of the grid should be at least 3 m (10 ft)—remember that any suspended lamp will be hanging below this. The preferred grid height is 3.6 m (12 ft). It offers a good lamp height, and it is reasonably easy to move equipment around. If the grid is above 4.2 m (14 ft) lamp-handling is more difficult.

Extra flexibility can be achieved by including a number of drop-arms or lightweight pantographs. The pantographs are more complex and expensive, but allow rapid adjustment of the luminaire height.

Heavy track suspension
This provides good flexibility. The basic arrangement consists of a number of heavy-duty tracks from which the luminaires are suspended on pantographs. A minimum studio height of 4.8 m (16 ft) is required. Each track is fitted with four luminaires which can be moved along it. The system is extremely flexible if the luminaires are dual source, i.e. spotlight/softlight. The spacing of the tracks must be such that two luminaires on adjacent tracks can pass each other. A track spacing of 1.2 m (4 ft) is a good compromise. Power is extended to the luminaires by a catenary system. The method for adding extra luminaires (e.g. for effects) depends on the type of track used. To allow for lighting from above a cyclorama, a peripheral lighting rail is added.

A development of this system is shown opposite (bottom) where the luminaires, on pantographs, slide on heavy-duty transverse tracks. The transverse tracks also slide in longitudinal tracks. This results in a readily adaptable lighting rig.

If the studio ceiling is not strong enough to take the weight of such suspension systems plus the luminaires, additional supporting steelwork may be built up from the studio floor in the form of tubular pole 'ladders'.

Suspension methods

1. Lighting grid. Cheap, easy to install and modify if requirements change. Most suitable for low ceiling heights.
2. *Drop arm* used to lower the lamp height by a fixed amount. Its length may be pre-adjusted.
3. *Telescopic drop arm* of adjustable length allows lamp height to be altered readily over a couple of feet.
4. *Pantographs* are adjustable over a wider range.

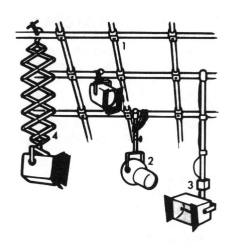

Ceiling power tracks

Heavy duty suspension tracks may span the ceiling, e.g. six tracks with four luminaires run on each track, powered from catenary tracks. They should be supplemented by a peripheral track.

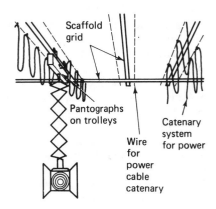

Scaffold grid

Pantographs on trolleys

Catenary system for power

Wire for power cable catenary

Adjustable lighting grid/lighting track

In this system part of the lighting grid is mounted on rollers which allow it to move in one direction. This produces a grid system which can be easily changed to meet each production's requirements. Ideally the luminaires should be suspended on trolley-mounted pantographs which run on the shorter moveable tracks. Again a peripheral track should be included, and consideration given to permanent cyclorama lighting from separate drop arms/pantographs.

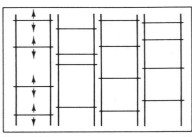

Short grid members move

Long grid members are fixed

Lighting: Outlets and Dimmers

The simplest form of lighting system is shown opposite. This is cheap, but not very flexible. In order to change the light intensity on a particular area the luminaire has to be moved, or the spot/flood mechanism has to be operated (on soft-edged spotlights). Alternatively, part of the luminaire lens can be obscured, for example by using 'wires' (Windolite) which reduce the light by approximately 25%, or the wattage (power-rating) of the lamp can be changed. Dual-wattage lamps provide alternative outputs by filament-switching.

Dimmers
Extra flexibility is obtained if a dimmer is used for every lighting circuit, as this will enable swift adjustment of lighting levels. Avoid using a patching system (see opposite) if possible. Note that 'switched-only' circuits will require special facilities on the lighting console. $2\frac{1}{2}$ kW dimmers should be adequate for a studio of less than 200 m² using modern cameras.

Number of outlets
How many outlets do we need, and where should they be situated? To decide on the number of power outlets we require, we need an estimate of the number of lamps we are likely to require in a given area.

A rough rule of thumb for the number of suspended luminaires required is 'one for every 3 m² (30 ft²) of studio area'. This should ensure sufficient luminaires for most programmes and avoid the need for too much movement of luminaires between programmes. The number required for say a 90 m² (900 ft²) studio would be 30 luminaires (say 20 hard sources and 10 soft sources).

The number of extra outlets to be included for special effects (e.g. pattern projectors) depends on the type of programmes envisaged, but generally 10 more outlets should be sufficient. If the cyclorama cloth is to be lit from above (not by a ground row), extra outlets should be included in the lighting grid.

Around the studio wall sufficient outlets should be included for lamps on the ground (e.g. ground rows for cyloramas and backdrops), for luminaires on stands and for 'practical' lamps (i.e. table lamps, wall brackets, and similar domestic fittings in the settings).

Phase
Where possible the power supply to the studio should be one phase. If more than one phase is used, for safety reasons it is essential that all floor outlets are on the same phase as the technical equipment.

Extensions
To allow for fixed power outlets to be extended, the studio should be equipped with a number of extension cables with single and multi-way distribution boxes. These should have robust plugs and sockets.

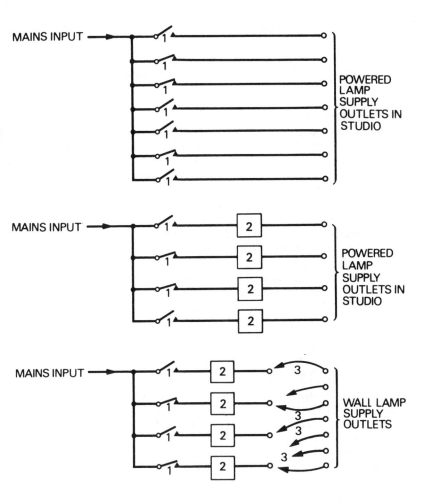

Switched-only lighting circuits
In this simple system, switched power (1) is available at all the lamp-supply sockets (outlets).

Dimmer circuits
Here each power channel incorporates a dimmer (2), to enable the intensity of its associated lamp(s) to be adjusted. A switch is usually included in each circuit.

Patching systems
In a cheaper more flexible system, a large number of lamp supply points (3) can be connected by a patching system, to a limited number of power points. (Wall outlets into which lamps plug are not powered until patched.)

Lighting: General-purpose Luminaires

The general-purpose luminaires required are soft-edged spotlights and soft sources.

Soft-edged spotlights

The fresnel spotlight produces a soft-edged beam of light which can be adjusted from narrow angle (spotted) to wide angle (flooded). In the fully flooded condition it behaves like a point source and produces hard-edged shadows. It is a good modelling light and can be used as a keylight, backlight and for scenic lighting.

The luminaire should be fitted with *barndoors* which are used to restrict the area illuminated. The barndoors are most effective in controlling the shape of the light beam when the luminaire is fully flooded.

In colour studios twin filament lamps may be used. These give added intensity adjustment because a luminaire can now provide a wide range of illumination values at a reasonably high colour temperature. Fresnel spotlights are available in a wide range of maximum wattages: 150 W (inky-dink), 500 W (pup), 1 kW, 2 kW, 5 kW, 10 kW and 20 kW.

Soft sources

A soft source is one which produces diffuse, shadowless light. To achieve this it needs to have a large area, which can be obtained in several ways:

● By using a frosted or opal bulb in an open reflector (scoop).

● By grouping together many internal reflector (sealed beam) lamps in one housing, e.g. 10-lite, mini-brute, nest.

● By grouping linear sources (strip lights) in a housing with suitable reflectors. This is used in colour studios and allows for dual wattage operation by switching out opposite pairs of light sources.

● Bouncing a hard source of light off a suitable reflector, e.g. polystyrene sheet.

Soft sources are not usually fitted with barndoors, so to reduce the sideways spread of light the units are fitted with spill rings or louvred openings.

For ease in setting the luminaire, pole-operated controls can be fitted. These adjust the spot/flood mechanism (on spotlights), pan and tilt functions, and the operating wattage on dual wattage luminaires. Luminaires used in colour studios should have a means of fixing colour media (colour filters) in front of them.

Tungsten halogen light sources used in many of these luminaires have the advantages (over normal tungsten sources) of longer life and a more compact envelope which does not darken during its life.

Open luminaires have the advantage that they use high-efficiency lamps, are small and lightweight, but the disadvantage that barndoors are not very effective in shaping the light beam.

Fresnel spotlight

Soft-edged spotlight, typically the beam angle can be varied from 12° (spot) to 60° (flood). Controls can be pole operated from the studio floor.

1. Pan
2. Tilt
3. Spot/flood (not visible)
4. Wattage switch

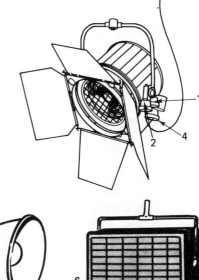

Soft sources

5. Scoop, using 500 watt or 1000 watt lamps.
6. 10 lite, using 10 × 150 W/200 W overrun reflector lamps.
7. Typical soft source using 2 × 1$\frac{1}{4}$ kW linear sources which may be switched off. Note louvre (8) and pole operation mechanism (9).

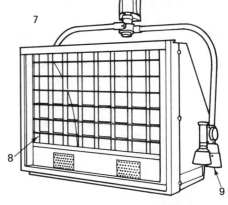

Open luminaires

10. 800 watt lightweight flood.
11. 1250 watt broad source.
12. Clamps to attach lightweight lamps to scenery.

Safety Note: Open luminaires should *not be used without a front protective glass or fine mesh* (2 mm), to avoid accidents if a bulb should explode.

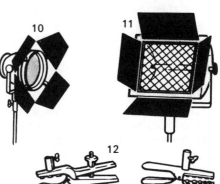

99

Lighting: Special Luminaires

These can be categorised as luminaires used for cyclorama lighting and for special effects lighting.

Cyclorama lighting

The most efficient method is to use luminaires especially designed for this purpose. A ground row produces a 'natural' effect, i.e. lighter at the horizon, with gradual reduction in illumination towards the top of the cyc. The multi-unit allows for colour mixing on a white cyc. The disadvantage of the ground row is the studio floor space it takes up, and the need to hide the lighting units behind suitable scenery (coving). Alternatively there are suspended luminaires available designed to produce even illumination of the cyclorama from top to bottom. These have the advantage of leaving a clear floor—very useful in a small studio.

Special effects lighting

The hard-edged projector can be used to project an image of a brightly illuminated circular aperture *or* the profile of any inserted metal stencil or mask. It can project a considerable variety of sharp or defocused images to add interest to an otherwise plain background. It can be fitted with internal metal shutters, which shape the beam with precision to light a defined area.

Hard-edged projectors are available with 500 W, 1 kW, 2 kW and 2.5 kW light sources. The projectors most suited to small studio operations are those which have a variable beam angle of 22°–36° or (for short-throw applications) 30°–45°.

Transparency projectors are used to project still or moving effects, e.g. clouds, water ripple, flames, etc. High-definition lenses are required for still projection, but for moving effects satisfactory results are obtained with a simpler lens system. Projector lenses of focal length 50, 75, 100 and 150 mm (2, 3, 4 and 6 in) give flexibility in throw and image size. When using these projectors, or any video projector, do make sure that the projected images will be bright enough.

Effects luminaires for pop/disco lighting are continually being developed. It is recommended that, except for PAR cans, all disco-type effects are hired for each production. The PAR can has many uses in addition to those of pop/disco, e.g. a 1 kW PAR can has the approximate candlepower of a 5 kW 'spotted' Fresnel spotlight and is extremely useful for bouncing off reflector boards.

Sophisticated moving lights are probably beyond the scope of operation and budget of small studios, however, simple Scrollers could be useful hired-in items for the right occasion, e.g. pop groups. Scrollers are fixed to the front of the luminaire and enable a roll of 11 or 16 coloured gel segments to be 'scrolled' through the light beam, thus giving a wide choice of projected colour.

Cyclorama lighting

1. Ground row containing 4 x 625 Watt linear lamps. For monochrome TV, units spaced 1.2 m (4 ft) apart should be adequate.
2. Suspended luminaire for lighting a cyc uniformly from above. Available in 1, 2, 3 and 4 unit form. Each has 625 Watt or 1.25 kW linear light sources

Hard-edged projector

3. 1 kW 'silhouette' projector with adjustable beam angle 22°-36°.
4. Slot for metal cut out or gobo.
5. Holder for colour media.
6. Beam-shaping shutters.

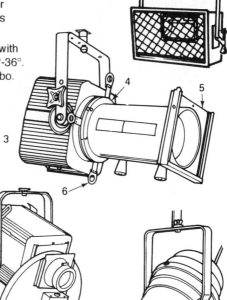

Transparency projectors

7. 2 kW projector for $3\frac{1}{4}$ x $3\frac{1}{4}$ inch still slides.
8. 2 kW projector for moving effects, e.g., clouds, fire, rain, smoke, etc., from a revolving glass disc.

PAR cans

9. PAR cans beam light available in 300 Watt and 1 kW sizes, with very narrow, narrow, medium and wide angle spread of light beam.
10. PAR can with stroller. This can be controlled from any lighting console providing 0-10V DC or DMX control signal. (See lighting console.)

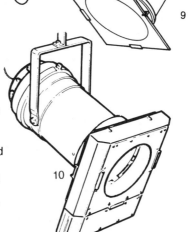

101

Lighting: Fluorescent Lights

The use of high-frequency fluorescent lights has been gaining popularity as an alternative light source because they are user-friendly and economic.

Why fluorescent lighting?
Fluorescent lighting has two major advantages over tungsten, namely
- Better efficiency, or more correctly efficacy, producing 3–4 times more light for each watt of electrical power.
- Little heat radiated in the light beam.

Recently, following the dramatic reduction in illumination requirements, the development of fluorescent tubes with acceptable colour rendition and the development of suitable fluorescent fixtures have made the fluorescent light source viable in television.

It should be remembered that any saving in lighting power is reflected in the air-conditioning plant size and its power consumption. Typically, the power requirements will be approximately 25% of that required if tungsten were to be used.

Comfortable artistes
With little or no radiant heat the presenters are more comfortable than when lit with tungsten (over 50% of the power is radiated in the beam!). It follows that less make-up repairs are required. The use of large-area sources also reduces glare for the presenters.

High-frequency operation
These fixtures operate at frequencies greater than 28kHz, resulting in greater efficiency compared to mains frequency operation and with no flicker problems; the light has effectively a constant light output, with little ripple, less than 0.1%. The latter ensures that the artistes have no problems of eye strain normally encountered with mains frequency fluorescents and camera shutters can be used without any strobing type effects. These units can be dimmed (currently to less than 20%) with little change in colour temperature.

Colour temperature and colour rendition
By using different phosphor coatings on the fluorescent tubes, a wide range of colour temperatures, from 2700 K to 6000 K, is available. This is yet another advantage of using fluorescent lights—one can choose a colour temperature appropriate to the application, e.g. to match tungsten sources or to match daylight with little or no colour correction. When using in-shot monitors (colour temperature normally 6500 K), selecting a high colour temperature studio white point will reduce the need for excessive colour correction on the monitor.

The colour rendition of a light source is measured with reference to either tungsten quality, or daylight if above 5000 K, on a scale from 0 to 100 (tungsten and daylight measuring 100). For television purposes the colour rendition index should be greater than 70, modern fluorescent tubes have colour rendition indices greater than 80 and sometimes 90, which are therefore capable of producing good quality television pictures.

Fluorescent lights

Range of fixtures available: 24 W - 832 W
Using range of lamps: 26 W, 36 W, 55 W compact 40 W tubular
Colour temperatures available: 2700 K, 3000 K, 4100 K, 5000 K and 5600 K
Dimmable ballasts: 0-10 V d.c. control signal using integral dimmer,
    or in some cases with conventional Thyristor dimmer

Typical fixtures

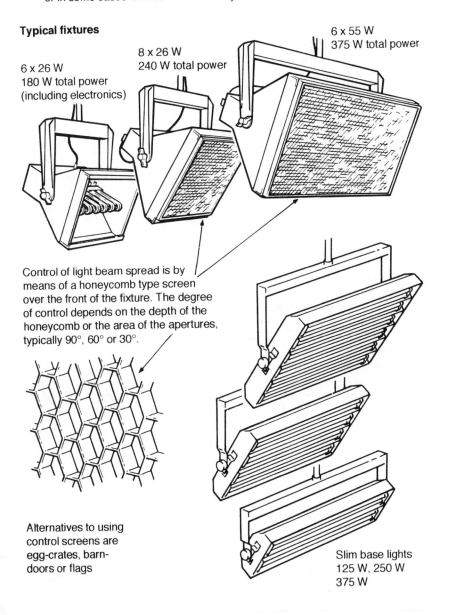

6 x 55 W
375 W total power

8 x 26 W
240 W total power

6 x 26 W
180 W total power
(including electronics)

Control of light beam spread is by
means of a honeycomb type screen
over the front of the fixture. The degree
of control depends on the depth of the
honeycomb or the area of the apertures,
typically 90°, 60° or 30°.

Alternatives to using
control screens are
egg-crates, barn-
doors or flags

Slim base lights
125 W, 250 W
375 W

Lighting Control: Dimmers (Analogue)

A dimmer is an electrical device used to control the light output from a luminaire. It should:

- Provide continuously variable control of the light output.
- Be easy to remotely control the dimmer with a simple fader.
- Dim the light progressively, with an appropriate law, which should not vary with the load, whether it be a 2 kW or 150 W lamp.
- Not be wasteful of power.
- Not cause interference to other equipment and be silent in operation.
- Be compact.
- Be easy to maintain.

Thyristor or SCR dimmers

The modern dimmer consists of two thyristors or silicon-controlled rectifiers (SCR) connected back-to-back as shown in figure C. The diodes do not conduct until switched on by a suitable pulse at the gate electrode (G). D_1 conducts on positive mains half-cycles and D_2 on negative mains half-cycles. The control voltage (0–10 V) on the fader is therefore used in a control amplifier to produce suitably delayed or advanced gating pulses. The voltage waveform to the lamp is therefore a chopped sinusoidal shape.

Interference

The thyristor dimmer satisfies most of the requirements listed above except one—interference. The very rapid switch-on of the load current can cause pulses of interference at 100 Hz (and harmonics of 100 Hz) on to adjacent microphone cables. This can also cause excessive vibrations of the lamp filament in the luminaire.

The interference can be reduced by:

- Including an inductor in the dimmer circuit. This reduces the rate of rise of the load current and results in reduced interference and less filament vibration.
- Using special screened quad cable for microphone circuits. This produces a marked decrease in interference pick-up (28 dB) and is used in many major TV studios.

Digital-multiplex control

Digital-multiplex control (DMX 512) enables a lighting console to provide a single control signal in digital form which can be decoded at the dimmer racks to provide the appropriate 0–10 V dimmer control signal for all the dimmers. This simplifies the distribution of control signals to the dimmers especially when used on location. The DMX 512 system can handle 512 dimmers and can also be used for control of moving lights and scrollers.

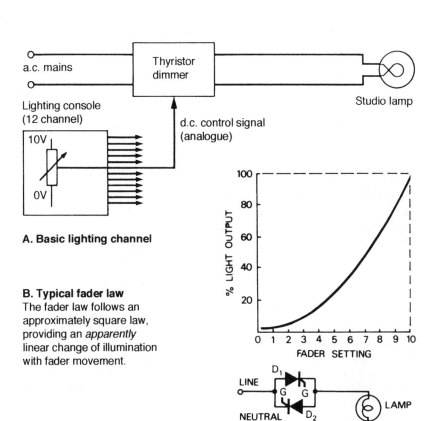

A. Basic lighting channel

a.c. mains

Lighting console
(12 channel)

10V

0V

Thyristor
dimmer

Studio lamp

d.c. control signal
(analogue)

B. Typical fader law

The fader law follows an
approximately square law,
providing an *apparently*
linear change of illumination
with fader movement.

% LIGHT OUTPUT

FADER SETTING

C. Silicon-controlled rectifiers

1. Waveform of the sinusoidal mains
   voltage applied to the silicon
   controlled rectifiers D_1 and D_2.
2. Waveform of the gating pulses
   applied to switch the SCR gate (G).
3. Resultant load-current waveform.

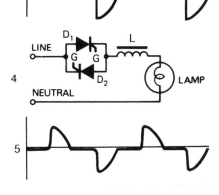

D. Reducing interference

4. Basic SCR dimmer circuit with
   the inductor (L) included for
   interference suppression.
5. Waveform of the load current,
   showing the effect of the
   inductor on the rise time of
   the current.

105

Lighting Control: Dimmers (Digital)

The use of micro-computer consoles and DMX 512 control signals has led to the development of the digital dimmer, using a digital system from the console to the processing of the control signal in the dimmer. Except for very basic installations all future dimming systems will use digital dimmers, which afford sophisticated control and improved reliability.

Advantages of digital dimmers
- Cheap (should remove the need for a patch panel).
- Better control of regulation (consistent law).
- Faster response time to required lighting changes.
- Processing in dimmer to give required dimmer law.
- DMX protocol operation.
- High reliability with consistent performance.
- Protection against overloads and short-circuits.
- Monitoring of dimmer load, control status and temperature.

Rack mounting
Thyristor dimmers are normally rack mounted in cabinets which have forced ventilation to prevent them overheating. Excessive heat causes the thyristors to function in an unpredictable manner and eventually to stop rectifying. The dimmers may be 'hard-wired', i.e. permanently connected or mounted in a plug-in unit. The latter method, although more expensive, allows for the swift replacement of a faulty dimmer.

Portable dimmers
If your operation involves a mixture of studio and location work portable dimmers could provide the necessary lighting control. These are compact packs, usually of $12 \times 2\frac{1}{2}$ kW, which may be stacked on site. In addition to operating with DMX or analogue signals these units normally have local dimming control on the dimmer pack.

A. Typical digital dimmer rack with plug-in dimmer modules
Each module has 2 x 2½ kW dimmers. This rack contains a maximum of 90 x 2½ kW dimmers.

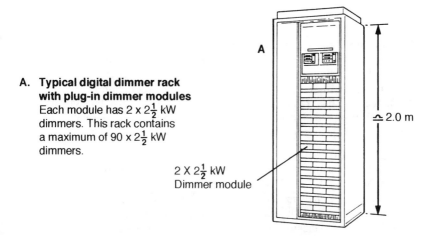

2 X 2½ kW
Dimmer module

≏ 2.0 m

B. Rack mounted dimmer pack using 'hard-wired' dimmers
12 x 2½ kW digital dimmers, in a standard 19" rack, or available as a portable unit (C) which may be flight case mounted

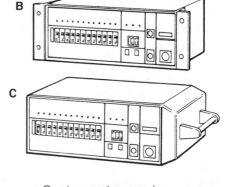

D. Example of typical facilities on a 12 channel digital dimmer pack

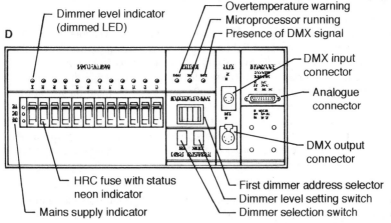

Dimmer level indicator (dimmed LED)

Overtemperature warning
Microprocessor running
Presence of DMX signal

DMX input connector

Analogue connector

DMX output connector

HRC fuse with status neon indicator

First dimmer address selector
Dimmer level setting switch
Dimmer selection switch

Mains supply indicator

107

Lighting Console

The function of the lighting console is to enable the lighting director to:
● Swiftly adjust the light output from the luminaires in use and so achieve a good *lighting balance* (i.e. appropriate relative intensities).
● Carry out any lighting changes required by the production.
● Reduce the heat build-up in the studio and power used, by switching out luminaires not immediately required. This also reduces the possibility of light spilling from adjacent sets.

Console design
The lighting console should be located in the vision control area. It should preferably:
● Be compact to facilitate one-man operation.
● Offer switching and brightness control on all the lighting channels.
● Be designed to facilitate productional lighting changes.
● Provide facilities for the quick selection and switching of a group of channels (memory system).
● Provide lighting effects, e.g. chasers, flickers, sound-to-light.
● Allow blind-plotting, i.e. creation of a lighting plot without affecting studio lighting.
● Be user-friendly i.e. easy and logical to operate.

Manual consoles
The simplest console design has two faders (or presets) per lighting channel, providing two lighting conditions controlled via two group master faders. Cross-fading between the groups can be manual or a timed dipless auto-crossfade. A Grand Master fader gives overall control of the lighting condition. An extension of this console would be the inclusion of special effects facilities, e.g. chase, flicker, sound-to-light etc. and the facility for 0–10 V analogue control signals or DMX control signals.

Computer consoles
There are many micro-processor controlled consoles available which offer extremely versatile control of lighting conditions, moving lights and scrollers. 'Soft-patch' of faders to dimmers enable many dimmers to be controlled by a few faders. Memories which store channel intensity give the facility for presetting lighting plots (at least 100) and control their recall (lighting changes). In most computer consoles the many rows of faders are replaced with a few faders and a key-pad for channel/memory selection. They include a VDU to give display of channel levels, memories in use, timing information etc. Usually, these consoles provide a DMX control signal as standard, with an optional analogue 0–10 V.

Load meter
Finally, a load meter should be included near the lighting console to indicate the production lighting power consumption. It should have an indication of the maximum permissible load.

A. Simple manual console

Typical 12 channel manual console, providing the facility of presetting two lighting conditions and cross-fading between them. Also available in 18 and 24 channel versions.

B. Manual console with effects

12 or 24 channel available, this console provides the additional features of 12 or 24 effects, e.g. chase, flicker, etc, with DMX or analogue control systems.

C. Computer console

This microcomputer based console provides 24 channels/1 preset, or 12 channels/2 presets with soft patch of 96 dimmers, 999 memories, 24 effects, DMX output (analogue option), comprehensive monitoring of lighting conditions with LCD display.

D. Computer console and VDU

This type of console typically has 120 or 240 channels controlling via a soft patch up to 512 dimmers, allocation of dimmer law (from 9), storage of a complete show on a cue card, 24 sub-masters, independant DMX output for control of scrollers, 24 programmable chasers, 20 special effects, 255 memories, 2 submasters studio/preset, blind plotting VDU display.
Options include infra-red control (from studio floor).

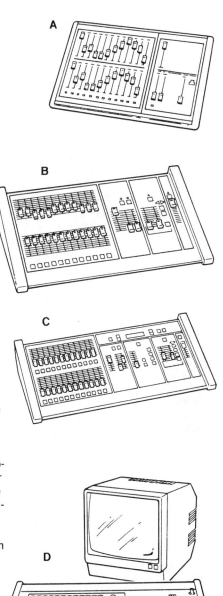

109

Microphone Assessment

Before buying microphones it is obviously necessary to take all reasonable steps to ensure that those purchased will be satisfactory. Below is a checklist of questions which, while not complete, should go some way towards helping buyers to obtain the most satisfactory microphones for their requirements.

Technical characteristics

Is the frequency response graph satisfactory and, more important, is the audio quality adequate as judged by listening tests using a high-grade loudspeaker?

What is its directivity pattern (see page 112) and how constant are its directional characteristics with frequency? Is the pattern variable—say by a switch on the microphone? What electrical load does the microphone require, and is this compatible with your existing equipment? How sensitive is it? Does moving the microphone produce unacceptable rumbles in the output, and how prone is it to wind noise? Are windshields available and if so how effective are they? If the microphone is to be used out of doors it is important that it is not affected by humidity. Check with the manufacturer whether it is prone to moisture problems.

Mechanical characteristics

Does the microphone appear rugged and well made? Is the cable-entry robust and likely to withstand pulling, and is the plug itself robust? What microphone-stand and sound-boom adaptors are available? What thread sizes do these have? How big and how heavy is the microphone? Is its appearance likely to be satisfactory if it is seen in shot? Is the finish shiny and therefore likely to cause 'flaring' in the picture? In the case of electrostatic microphones, are the capsules interchangeable? Are there extension tubes?

Powering arrangements

All electrostatic (including electret microphones) need a power supply. The most common professional way is to use the three-conductor microphone cable to carry this as well as the audio signal. This is known as 'phantom-powering'; the standard voltage is nominally 48 V. However, other systems exist. What system does the microphone under consideration use? Is it compatible with your other microphones? Alternatively, can batteries be used, how many hours use can be expected from each, and are they readily obtainable?

Makers and cost

Are the manufacturers well known? Do they have local agents? What do you know of their spares and repair service? What guarantees do they give? How long has the microphone you are considering been in production? Is it likely to go out of production in the near future?

How much does it cost and does this include cables and power units? How expensive are the accessories?

Typical data for a good quality microphone

Transducer	Electrostatic using FET.
Directivity pattern	Cardioid capsule normally supplied but interchangeable with other capsules, e.g. omni, gun.
Power supplies	48 V d.c. *Phantom* power. Battery unit using 9 V battery, with battery life of 40 hours.
Impedance	Nominally 200 Ω balanced output. Minimum load impedance 500 Ω.
Sensitivity	−39 dB rel. to 1 V/N/m² (−59 dB rel. to 1 V/dyne/cm²).
Connectors	3-pin DIN or XLR type, as ordered.

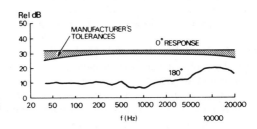

**Frequency response
(cardioid capsule)**

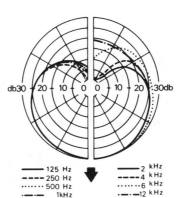

**Directivity pattern
(cardioid capsule)**

Accessories	Mounting swivel bracket. 'Gun' tube. Pistol grip for 'gun'. 30 mm and 130 mm extension tubes. Foam and metal mesh windshields.
Dimensions	147 mm long, 18 mm diameter.
Weight	120 g.
Finish	Matt.

111

Microphone Categories

The directivity pattern (or polar diagram) of a microphone indicates its response to sounds from different directions. The most important directivity patterns are given below.

Omni-directional
Sound pick-up is normally independent of angle of incidence but in fact this is only the case at the lower frequencies (typically below 2–4 kHz). Except as 'personal' microphones (e.g. for use with radio microphone systems) the use of omni-directional microphones is limited in television studios because of their inability to reject reverberation and general studio noise.

Cardioid
These are widely used because, when pointed at an artiste or presenter, their 'dead' sides are likely to be directed towards areas of noise in the studio. They also reject a significant amount of reverberation.

Figure-of-eight
These are relatively little used in television work but they may have occasional application in out-of-vision situations where the 'dead' sides can be used to reject unwanted sounds. A well-known type of 'noise-cancelling' microphone—the so-called 'lip-ribbon', much used for commentaries—has a figure-of-eight response, although its rejection of external sounds depends on other properties.

Hypercardioid
This is a pattern half-way between figure-of-eight and cardioid, and can often be useful when the unwanted noises are neither at the rear nor at the sides. The frontal angle of pick-up is narrower than that of a cardioid. This can be an advantage in some instances, a drawback in others.

Gun microphones
So called because of their shape, there are basically two types: 'short' guns with a tube about 25 cm long, and the longer variety with a tube length of around 50 cm. The short guns usually have a directivity pattern which is not unlike a hypercardioid and is sometimes described as such by the makers. The longer microphones have an angle of pick-up at high frequencies of about 30°. This broadens as the frequency decreases to being, in a typical case, approximately cardioid at low frequency. The longer gun microphones rarely perform well in small rooms.

Variable directivity
Inevitably these are relatively expensive. However, the cost may be justified because, by operation of a switch, either on the body of the microphone or on a remote box, the directivity pattern can be changed from omni-directional to cardioid, to figure-of-eight or intermediate patterns (but *not* gun).

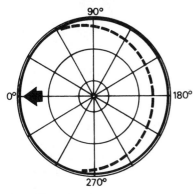

Omnidirectional
Sensitivity is more-or-less equal all round.

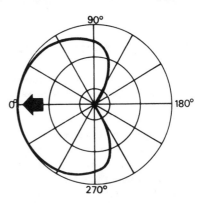

Cardioid
Some degree of directionality is introduced to produce a heart-shaped response curve.

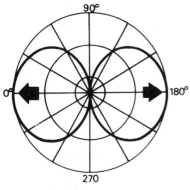

Figure-of-eight
Bi-directional sensitivity allows equal response in opposite directions.

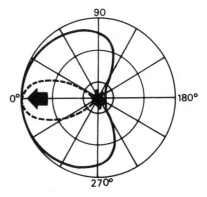

Highly directional
Special constructions, such as the gun microphone, allow small sources to be pinpointed.

Hypercardioid
Has dead points about 45° off the rear.

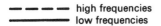
high frequencies
low frequencies

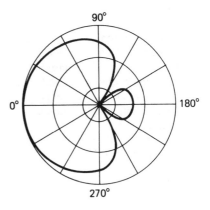

Sound Pick-up

There are various ways of supporting microphones in a television studio. Some of the very important are set out below.

Boom

This is easily the most versatile method. With it, an experienced operator can position a microphone with great accuracy at any angle and at any position in a large area. However, booms are expensive and it can take months or even years for a boom operator really to learn the art. Furthermore a large space is needed for the benefits of a boom to be gained, so this often precludes their use in small studios.

Fishpole

This is a rudimentary but nevertheless useful form of boom. It consists of a length of light rod (stout bamboo is satisfactory) with the microphone fixed to one end. The rod is normally 2–3 metres long. An advantage of the fishpole is that, unlike the boom, it can be used below the level of a presenter's head and still be out of shot. Operator fatigue can be a problem with long takes.

Stand microphones

Stands tend to be unacceptably obtrusive in shot, except perhaps for some musical programmes. However, they should form part of every studio's equipment for out-of-vision applications.

Personal microphones

These can be quite unobtrusive and can give great freedom of movement to a presenter. It is often possible to conceal such a microphone completely beneath clothing, but problems can occur from static and clothing rustles (see page 112).

Slung microphones

It is sometimes possible to get very satisfactory sound coverage from microphones hanging over the set. Be careful to avoid perspective problems—from, for example, a presenter beneath a slung microphone walking towards camera but getting further from the microphone.

Microphone positioning

A few general points, applicable to both fishpoles and booms are:
1. As a rough guide a microphone at arm's length and at 45° to the speaker's mouth should give reasonable results. Depending on the acoustic environment, greater working distances are possible with gun microphones.
2. The position of lights should be noted to avoid shadows of the microphone appearing in the picture.
3. The sound operator must note all camera positions, zoom angles etc. to ensure that the microphone never appears in shot.

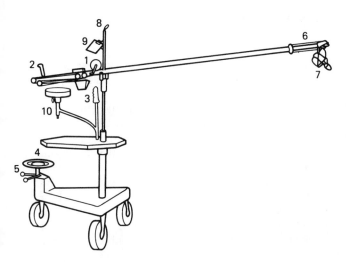

Microphone boom

The boom arm's length (3–6 metres) is adjusted by a wheel (1), and pivoted in its central cradle. The microphone can be titled and rotated by a control lever (2). The overall height of the boom arm and platform can be adjusted (3) between 1 and 1.5 m. The boom pram is steerable (4) and can be held stationary by a brake (5). (6) Extending section. (7) Microphone in cradle. (8) Talk-back microphone. (9) Script board. (10) Seat.

Fishpole

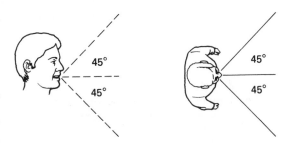

Acceptable sound pick-up angles

Radio Microphone

The term radio microphone is usually something of a misnomer because in most cases the microphone itself is a conventional device. It is simply fed into a miniature transmitter/receiver system.

The advantage of the radio microphone is that a performer can move freely over a relatively large area without the hindrance of trailing cables.

There are two drawbacks to radio microphones. One is their relatively high cost and the second is that they are inevitably less reliable than a conventional microphone cable. With modern electronics the reliability is normally good, but care has to be taken to avoid areas in the studio where pick-up is poor because of radio blackout or interference. In the VHF band used by most devices there is always a risk of 'multipath' interference or screening by metal structures. Consequently in setting up for a programme, it is advisable to check carefully all the anticipated positions of the microphone's transmitter, and choose carefully the siting of the receiver aerial. We should not overlook, too, that trouble can arise when a camera moves into the vicinity of either transmitter or receiver, so during rehearsal a member of the crew should be available to reposition the receiver. (Diversity reception systems can reduce the risks of 'black-out' regions.)

Battery life
A miniature transmitter must contain small batteries and consequently the operating life of the batteries is fairly short, even with the modest powers radiated by most transmitters of this type. A life of 4–6 hours is typical. It is usually good practice to put new batteries in the transmitter for each programme (assuming the bare minimum of an hour or two's rehearsal followed by the transmission or recording).

Interference
It is advisable, when buying radio microphones, to check that there are no local sources of serious radio interference on the same frequency as that of the intended purchase. The limited range of the average transmitter makes it unlikely that it would interfere with other services or equipment, but the converse situation could be, at worst, disastrous. If two or more radio microphones are used it is essential that each operates on a different frequency.

Hiring
In the UK there are commercial organisations which hire out radio microphones on a daily basis. Bearing in mind the high cost of buying these items, hiring should be looked into if they are going to be used infrequently.

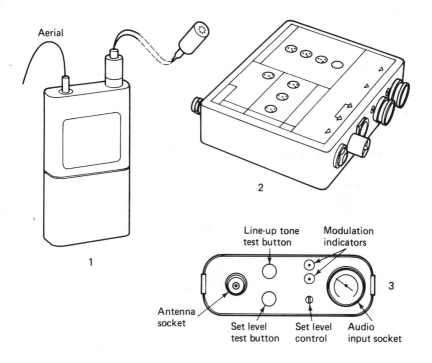

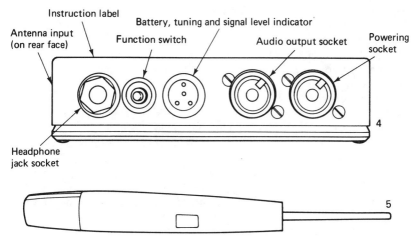

Radio microphone equipment
1. Transmitter.
2. Receiver.
3. Transmitter top panel.
4. Receiver front panel.
5. Hand held radio microphone.

Sound Mixing Consoles

A mixing console basically provides the following facilities:

● Control of the level of the output audio signal so that it is neither so weak as to be audibly near to background noise, nor so high as to risk distortion in subsequent stages (e.g. recording).

● Balancing the outputs of sources such as microphones, effects, tape, disc etc. to give an artistically suitable mix.

● Allow processing of the audio signal(s), i.e. addition of echo (page 128), frequency correction (use of EQ, page 126) etc.

Basic design

The diagram opposite shows some of the essential features of a sound mixing console but omitting all amplifiers. Essentially each source is connected to an input socket, often of the XLR type. The channel faders control the level of each source, while the group faders act as sub-master controls. The insertion points (pairs of jacks) may be found not just as shown but also after the channel faders and possibly in the groups as well. Their purpose is to allow extra devices such as limiter/compressors (page 124) to be inserted into the chain.

Operational facilities

In addition to the features mentioned above, the following are very important in each channel.

● Preset gain—a small potentiometer, switched or continuously variable, or both, to allow the channel to accept a range of input levels from, say, −80 dB to +20dB.

● Equalisation (EQ) and filters (page 126).

● Echo control—to control the amount of channel signal sent to an echo device (page 128).

● Foldback and PA level controls (page 120).

● Prehear (PFL) and afterfade listen (AFL) to allow checks on the level and quality of a source before or after it has been faded up.

Note: the facilities above may be found associated with groups as well with channels.

Additional features of a console include:

● Echo return fader and echo monitoring.

● Monitoring of the signal by both meters (page 122) and loudspeakers (page 130).

● 'Clean feed' ('mix-minus') outputs (page 120).

● Stereo facilities, which are becoming increasingly important in television sound.

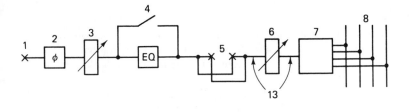

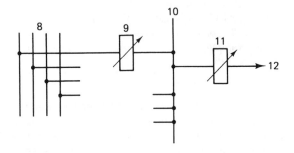

Simplified sound mixing console
 1. Channel input socket.
 2. Phase reverse switch.
 3. Channel sensitivity control (also switches impedance from about 1.2 kΩ for microphone level inputs to 6–10 kΩ for line level inputs).
 4. EQ bypass switch.
 5. Insert points.
 6. Channel fader.
 7. Channel routing.
 8. Group busbars.
 9. Group fader.
10. Main busbar.
11. Main fader.
12. Output.
13. Auxiliaries (see pages 110, 111).

Sound Mixing Console: Outputs

The main programme output of the sound console is fed to the VT machine or the transmission network. More sophisticated designs of sound mixing console include additional auxiliary outputs, foldback, public address and clean feed.

Foldback

Here one or more selected sources are fed to loudspeakers on the studio floor. On most sound consoles, the volume (level) of the foldback is controllable on the console. The most common function of foldback is to provide audible cues to performers.

A feed of telecine sound played over the studio foldback loudspeaker, for example, not only provides audible cues for the end of the film sequence, but also gives an indication of pace and delivery. There is often a need to give members of an out-of-vision band individual feeds of foldback via headphones. These will typically be mixes of other sections of the band. A vocalist might, for example, want a headphone foldback of one or two melodic instruments plus rhythm.

Public address

Essentially similar, electrically, to foldback, the PA feed is taken to loudspeakers in the vicinity of a studio audience. It can generally be assumed that a studio audience will be unable to hear much of the direct sound from the studio floor. Consequently reinforcement of this sound is essential if the audience is to be able to hear properly and thus be able to react—i.e. laugh, applaud, etc. Directional (line-source) loudspeakers are normally needed to prevent inadvertent pick-up of the PA sound by studio microphones. These require careful positioning and suitable gain settings if 'howl-rounds' and 'colouration' are to be avoided.

The balance of the PA feed is generally different from that of the main console output. For example, the backing group for a vocalist may require little PA reinforcement but the sound of the vocalist will probably need considerable amplification.

Clean feed (mix-minus)

Using 'clean feed' circuits, we can selectively omit certain chosen sound sources, while listening to the studio output. For example, in a music mix musicians might wish to hear on their headphones only the rhythm section. They would then be given a clean feed—in this case the console output *less* all sources except the microphones on the rhythm section (in practice auxiliary outputs from the rhythm microphones).

Clean feeds are also important if two or more studios are being used simultaneously with contributions from each. Clean feeds can ensure that each studio loudspeaker reproduces only the output from the *other* studio. In this way the risk of howl-round and unwanted colouration is greatly reduced.

120

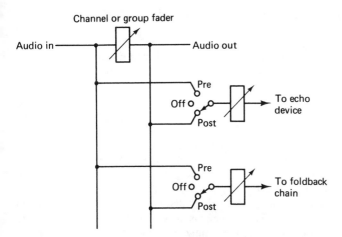

Simplified diagram of foldback and PA circuits

If a PA or foldback system is fed from a point *before* a channel fader it will only be influenced by the system's controls, and not by fader operation. (Otherwise channel fader readjustments necessitate rebalancing the system—e.g. to prevent howl-round.) The channel fader often incorporates a switch cutting the PA circuit when the control is faded out (backstop).

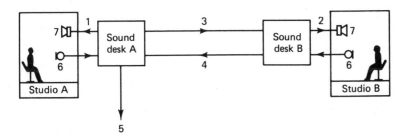

Clean feed and two-way working

To avoid echo or howl-round effects, circuit arrangements are made for a contributor to hear a feed from the other studio, of all sounds *except* his own output. This simplified illustration outlines the method used.

1. Studio B sound only.
2. Studio A sound only.
3. Clean feed of Studio A sound.
4. Clean feed of Studio B sound.
5. Studio A+Studio B sound.
6. Microphones.
7. Loudspeakers.

121

Monitoring Sound Levels

Sound signals from a mixing desk need to be monitored in two ways:
- Using a high-grade loudspeaker for assessment of quality, balance, etc.
- Using a suitable electrical indicator to check that the sound signal is within the prescribed limits of the system.

VU meter
The commonest indicator is the VU (volume unit) meter, which is a voltmeter of suitable ballistic and impedance characteristics, connected across the circuit to be monitored. Although cheap, the VU meter has the drawback that it cannot register short-duration signal peaks with any accuracy, although these peaks can cause undesirable overload distortion in amplifiers, recording equipment, transmitters, etc. Such a meter is nevertheless perfectly satisfactory for line-up purposes when steady tones only are involved.

Peak programme meter
Much more satisfactory devices for visual monitoring of audio signals than the VU meter are those based on the peak programme meter (PPM) designed originally by the BBC.

A PPM consists basically of two parts: a peak-detector with a logarithmic amplifier and a display device. Until a few years ago the only available type of display was a high-grade moving-coil meter. More recently various types of LED or plasma display have been available. The latter have the advantage of occupying less space on a console, and different colours can be used to indicate, say, imminent overload. On the other hand a conventional meter can sometimes be easier to read and may be more accurate when reading steady levels as, for example, in lining up equipment. (For stereo work a pair of coaxially mounted movements, giving a double pointer display, is often preferable to any other kind of display.)

It is part of the essential characteristics of a PPM device, no matter what type of display, that programme peaks are shown for long enough to be readable and also that the readings are proportional to decibels. For example, in the meter types the scale divisions are 4 dB apart, except at the bottom of the range. To reduce eye strain the meters have white pointers and white scale markings.

It must be noted that neither the PPM nor the VU meter can be used to give a reliable indication of sound loudness, and therefore cannot be used for any kind of measurement of sound balance.

Peak programme meter

A special type of voltmeter, with a simplified logarithmic scale (in 4 dB steps). It has a rapid rise characteristic and a slower die-away time. '4' on the scale represents zero level (40% modulation), '6' represents 100% modulation.

Volume units (VU) meter

The dual scale on the VU meter includes decibels indications, and a percentage modulation scale.

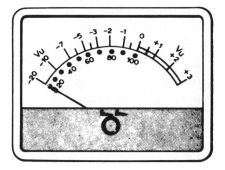

123

Automatic Level Control

It is often necessary to have some means of automatically controlling sound levels. For example, loud sounds, particularly in location work, cannot always be anticipated and overloads can occur because a fader has not been taken down sufficiently. It must be emphasised that automatic devices can never operate as intelligently as a human being, and if not used with discretion the results they produce can be unpleasant. However, used with care they can be very useful.

Compression

A compressor is a variable gain amplifier, the gain being set by the level of the input or output signal. The diagram opposite illustrates typical compressor characteristics. The most important are:

● *Threshold*—this is adjustable and determines the level above which gain reduction will occur.

● *Compression ratio*—a compression ratio of, say, 5:1 means that for an increase in input signal level of 5 dB *above the threshold* the *output* level will increase by only 1 dB. Similarly an increase of 10 dB above the threshold will cause the output to go up by 2 dB.

● *Recovery time* (*decay time, release time*)—a measure of the time taken for the gain to return to normal after compression has taken place. This is typically variable from several milliseconds to a few seconds. (Long recovery times preserve something of the original dynamic range but this can cause the 'loss' of important quiet sounds following immediately after loud ones. Short recovery times, on the other hand, can result in 'pumping'—the gain going up and down in level.)

● *Attack time*—the time for the device to respond. Values from less than 1 ms to 20–30 ms are typical. (Very short attack times prevent any peaks from going through the system but may affect sound quality adversely because of a modification of the transients.)

● *Limiting*—a high value of compression ratio. In practice this is usually at least 20:1 and may be much more. On some devices the threshold for limiting is automatically set to be 8dB above the threshold for compression.

Applications

These are too numerous to list, but two representative ones are:

● In the output of the console to protect against unexpected overloads causing distortion in subsequent equipment such as the sound channel of a video recorder.

● In a microphone channel to hold the level (volume) of one source more-or-less constant.

Noise Gates

These are in fact circuits providing expansion — the opposite of compression. A noise gate may be used to keep unwanted ambient noise such as ventilation at a much lower level than would otherwise be the case by keeping the noise signal below the vertical section in the graph opposite.

124

Simplified limiter/compressor
A side-chain circuit (1) samples the main programme signal, and modifies the performance of the main variable-gain amplifier (2) according to the control settings (compression ratio and recovery time). Dashed lines show the arrangement of the side chain in a 'feed forward' type of device.

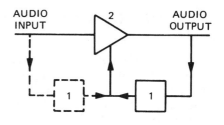

Basic parameters of a typical limiter/compressor
The limiter accommodates input levels over a range of −12 to +8 dB. Any signal exceeding a determined level (3) causes feedback that reduces the circuit gain, bringing it within the required limits.

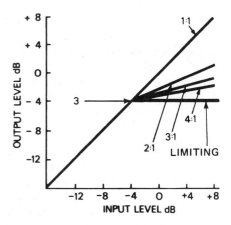

Simplified characteristics of a noise gate

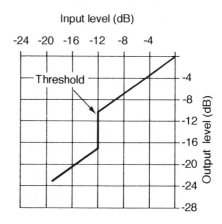

125

Frequency Correction

There are a number of occasions where we want to alter the frequency response of a channel in a sound desk for technical or artistic reasons:

● To match the response of one type of microphone with another, so that when cross-fading there is no obvious difference in quality.

● To match the quality of sound on a film insert to studio sound.

● To simulate effects such as telephone speech.

● To improve clarity by, for example, putting in bass-cut to reduce the effects of low-frequency reverberation.

● To compensate for the fact that a microphone has to be in a position where it cannot pick up optimum sound quality.

Types of correction

Frequency correction devices can be divided into several categories, although there are often no sharp divisions:

● *Console channel equalisers* (*EQ*). These normally provide variable amounts of bass lift and cut, and treble lift and cut. The turn-over frequency is often switchable. (See the diagram opposite.)

● *Filters*. These usually have a very steep slope (15–18 dB/octave) and provide bass cut and top cut. Typical uses are for removing microphone rumble and ventilation whistle.

● *Presence controls*. Often part of a console EQ system, these give mid-frequency lift and cut, usually at several switchable frequencies.

● *Parametric equalisers*. These differ from the types of equaliser listed above only in that frequencies are continuously variable instead of being switchable. This means, for example, that the frequency of an intrusive tone can be accurately located and at least partially 'tuned out'. A useful feature of many parametric equalisers is the facility to alter the sharpness ('Q') of the response curves.

● *Graphic equalisers*. Commonly these take the form of a set of slide faders, each one operating on a particular frequency band. The position of the fader knob above or below the centre line determines the amount of lift or cut at that frequency. Modestly priced devices have a control for each octave, while on more expensive ones each fader covers one-third of an octave.

Care in use

While frequency correction devices are invaluable adjuncts to sound mixing equipment, and are commonly incorporated in the channels of many sound desks, they must always be used with discretion. Inexperienced operators should avoid using them unnecessarily. It is better to try to get the sound right in the first place than to hope to improve it by frequency correction.

126

Typical equaliser curves
Although one normally aims for a flat frequency response overall, deliberate reduction or reinforcement of parts of the audio spectrum can improve reproduced sound quality.

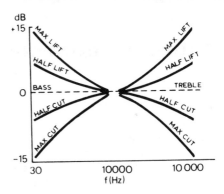

Presence filters
By boosting part of the audio spectrum, we can often enhance the illusion of subject clarity and separation. The illustration shows typical presence settings.

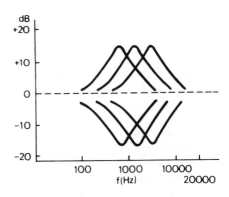

High-pass filters
These filter circuits introduce a fall-off in bass to reduce distracting rumble, hum, or low-pitched vibration pick-up.

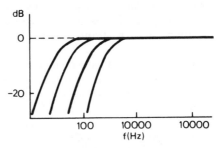

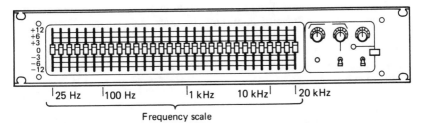

Frequency scale

Graphic equaliser
Here slide faders adjust the system's audio response curve to modify the resultant sound quality. This design permits +12 dB to −12 dB insertion at the frequencies indicated.

127

Artificial Reverberation

Why use it?
There are three basic reasons: (1) to simulate a particular acoustic environment, e.g. in a drama scene set in a church a relatively long reverberation time must be added to the recordings made in a studio; (2) in music, to enhance or 'sweeten' the sound, e.g. to simulate the acoustics of a concert hall; (3) for special musical or dramatic effects where there is no attempt at realism.

Artificial reverberation devices
In the past there have been several devices designed to simulate artificial reverberation. These have included 'echo' rooms, reverberation plates and special springs. Within the last decade digital reverberation units have become available at costs ranging from the equivalent of a pair of medium-priced microphones to ten or more times as much. However, even the low-priced models are capable of a very realistic simulation of reverberation.

Features of digital units
● The reverberation time can be varied from, typically, less than 1 second to 10 or more seconds. On the less expensive devices there may be a limited range of perhaps four settings.
● 'Predelay'. Aural assessment of an environment includes not only the reverberation time but also the time gap between the direct sound and the first reflections, often referred to as 'predelay'. This is variable on most digital reverberation units. In the simpler ones it may appear as a range of 'room sizes'.
● Early (and other) reflections. The acoustic quality of a room is affected by the more-or-less discrete reflections in the early stages of the reverberation. These can be simulated in many digital units and may be incorporated into programs which can be called up with specific names. Included among them is often a 'plate' program, for those who, as mentioned above, prefer the quality of plate reverberation.
● Filters. These alter the reverberation time/frequency characteristic.
● Storage of programs. The more expensive units contain memories so that particular settings of reverberation time, program, predelay and filters can be stored for rapid recall. This is particularly useful when the character of the artificial reverberation needs to be changed quickly. These memories are usually non-volatile so that switching off the unit does not wipe the contents of the memory.

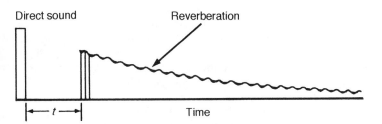

Direct sound | Reverberation

$\leftarrow t \rightarrow$ Time

'*t*' is the time for the first reflected sound to reach the listener after the arrival of the direct sound. If it is more than about 40 ms then the listener is aware of a time gap. If less than 30-40 ms the time interval is not conciously perceived but is nevertheless used by the listener to assess the apparent size of the room. Thus for correct simulation, say for drama purposes, of a particular-sized environment the choice of an appropriate 'pre-delay' is important.

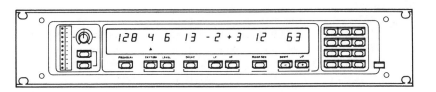

Digital reverberation unit
A typical unit with adjustable predelay and a choice of several reverberation simulations.

Loudspeakers

Broadly speaking, loudspeakers are used in television studios for several different purposes, such as monitoring, studio foldback, audience (PA), and intercommunication.

Monitoring

A high-quality monitoring loudspeaker in the sound-mixing area is essential. It must have a wide and flat frequency response and a good response to transients (the vitally important first few tens of milliseconds of a sound).

An easily overlooked fact is that the response of loudspeakers is apt to be affected by their proximity to walls, floors and ceilings. For this reason any loudspeaker being considered should, if possible, be listened to in the position in which it will be used. Other important factors are the power-handling (will it produce enough noise?) and the directional characteristics (very high-quality reproduction over a very narrow angle may be less desirable than slightly less good reproduction over a wider angle). Also the size and weight are significant factors.

An additional point to bear in mind is that it is desirable to have the same type of loudspeaker in all other production areas: production control room, post-dubbing and editing suites, and so on.

Studio loudspeakers

Studio-floor loudspeakers are employed both for general studio talkback and for foldback (page 120). Good quality loudspeakers should be used, although parameters are not so stringent as for monitoring purposes. Factors that are important here are portability (the loudspeaker should be mounted on a small trolley—with quiet castors!) and ruggedness. The ability to handle fairly large sound levels is desirable, although this may be required only very occasionally.

PA systems

Audience (PA) loudspeakers usually need to be directional to avoid their output being picked up by studio microphones. This directional radiation is provided in the 'line-source' ('column') type of loudspeaker. Line-source loudspeakers provide intelligible sound, but of an overall quality that is usually inferior to that expected from the best monitoring types.

Loudness

With monitoring loudspeakers there needs to be a balance between the ability of operators to listen for slight imperfections in the sound output and a level at which there is a risk of hearing impairment. A fairly large monitoring loudspeaker can produce noise levels of around 115–120 dBA at a distance of 1m. Such a unit at full volume can cause serious noise leakage into other areas unless acoustic insulation is very good. While the risk of hearing damage to staff in the control room is likely to be small the possible hazard should not be overlooked. It is generally accepted for example, that a continuous sound, level of 96 dBA for 2 hours a day should not be exceeded.

A maximum loudspeaker output of about 90 dBA at 1 m is probably quite adequate for typical small studio control rooms. This is well within acceptable limits for exposure and the loudspeaker output should not be so high as to cause undesirable sound leakage into adjacent areas.

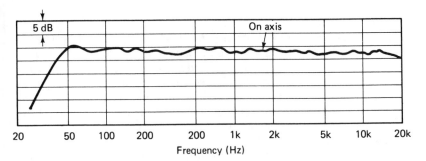

| 5 dB | | | | | On axis | | | |

Frequency (Hz)

20   50   100   200   200   1k   2k   5k   10k   20k

Studio loudspeakers
Frequency response of a high-grade monitoring loudspeaker.

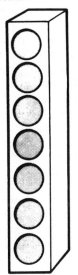

Line source loudspeaker
A columnar loudspeaker enclosure,
this provides a directional source,
enabling sound to be reproduced
over a narrow vertical angle,
without danger of pick-up by
nearby audience microphones.
The directivity pattern of the
enclosure is pronounced for
frequencies of wavelength less than
the length of the column.

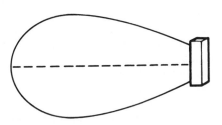

131

Audio Tape Recorders (Analogue)

One or more audio tape recorders are essential in the sound control area of any television studio. Typical usage includes introductory, play-out, and background music, spot sound effects, and 'off-stage' dialogue.

Types of recorder

Tape machines vary considerably in price, quality and range of facilities. A small cassette machine costs a fraction of the price of a high-quality professional reel-to-reel machine. Cassette machines are cheap, small, and easily handled, and cassettes are rapidly inserted and removed. On the other hand, their quality and background noise (signal-to-noise ratio) cannot equate with the heavier duty reel-to-reel type of machine, although more expensive cassette recorders may be sufficient for some purposes. Cartridge machines are good for jingles and effects.

Unlike simpler tape-recorders, a reel-to-reel machine with separate record and replay heads provides an immediate continual check of recording quality, because the output of the replay head can be fed to the monitoring loudspeaker. (All recordings should, if possible, be made using this facility.)

Desirable operational features

Operational experience has shown various features to be desirable in television studio tape machines including:

● Large (NAB type) spools giving, with standard tape, just over one hour's playing time at 19 cm/s. Removal of the centres to permit the playing of 'cine' spools should be quick and easy.

● Frequency response, wow and flutter characteristics should be well within specifications, and regular routine checks made. Machines get heavy use, and performance can deteriorate.

● The start/run-up time should be 'instantaneous', if accurately timed effects are to be introduced on cue.

● The stability of modern machines is very good but because the characteristics of different brands of tape vary it is desirable that the record and replay gain, the bias and the equalisation can be adjusted fairly easily, and this means reasonably accessible controls.

● There should be jacks for the headphone monitoring of both the record and replay signals, and it should be possible to have pre-fader listen so that a tape can be 'cued up' with the tape machine replay fader (if there is one) faded out.

● It should be easy to edit tape on the machine, i.e. to mark the tape with a suitable pencil at the position of the replay head and to spool with the tape in contact with the replay head.

● Although tape counters operated by the rotation of one of the idler wheels can be affected by tape slip it is still possible for them to be quite accurate (an error of only 1–2 seconds in half an hour). A good counter display (preferably digital showing hours, minutes and seconds) is an asset.

132

SPECIFICATION OF A HIGH QUALITY TAPE MACHINE

Tape speeds	38 and 19 cm/s ±0·2% (15 and 7½ in/s)
Tape slip	<0.1%
Wow and flutter	<0.05% at 38 cm/s <0.08% at 19 cm/s
Start time to reach speed (0.2% flutter)	<0.5s
Rewind time	120 s for 2400 ft reel
Max. input level	+22 dB
Max. undistorted output level	+24dB
Frequency response at 38 cm/s	30 Hz to 18 kHz±2 dB 60 Hz to 15 kHz±1 dB
at 19 cm/s	30 Hz to 15 kHz±2 dB 60 Hz to 12 kHz±1 dB
Overall signal-to-noise ratio	61 dB at 38 cm/s (full track) with CCIR equalisation
Erase efficiency	75 dB or better at 1 kHz
Bias and erase frequency	150 kHz

Audio Noise Reduction Systems

The upper end of the dynamic range of an audio system is normally the level at which distortion occurs because of overload. The lower end of the range is set by noise: tape hiss, 'thermal' noise in electronic components, mains hum, and so on.

The effects of such noise can be reduced very significantly by *noise reduction* systems, which are commonly used, particularly in analogue recording. (Digital systems are almost totally unaffected by the noise problems mentioned above.) Most noise reduction systems make use of some form of companders—that is, the dynamic range is reduced before recording or transmission etc. and expanded afterwards. Unfortunately simple compressors and expanders generally produce audible side effects. The more successful arrangements manage to avoid these effects.

Dolby A

This was the original system produced by the Dolby organisation and was intended to reduce the effects of noise on professional tape recording and also on long-distance audio transmission systems. The increased use of digital recording and transmission has made Dolby A less important, although it is still widely used in multitrack analogue machines. A brief account of it is worth giving as the other Dolby systems are based on it. The essential point is that it operates only on low-level signals, the argument being that high-level signals mask the effects of noise. Also it divides the audio frequency range into four bands which work independently of each other. This means that, for example, reasonably high-level low-frequency signals are not processed when the higher frequency end *does* contain low levels and is therefore processed. The Dolby A frequency bands are shown on the opposite page.

Because the Dolby A system operates only on low-level signals, line-up of 'send' and 'receive' (e.g. record and replay) is rather critical.

Other systems

● *Dolby B*. A low-cost method of reducing tape hiss on cassettes. It operates only on the higher frequencies and can result in about 10 dB of reduction of tape hiss.

● *Dolby C*. A more advanced form of Dolby B. It operates on two frequency bands and can give about 20 dB of noise reduction. It is frequently found on professional and the better domestic cassette decks.

● *Dolby SR* ('SR' = spectral recording). This is relatively recent. It is claimed that recording levels can be increased by 10 dB and there is around 24 dB reduction in tape noise.

● *dbx*. This consists of a compressor-expander pair working with a compression ratio of 2:1. It can provide up to 24 dB of noise reduction and does not need careful line-up. What noise does get through, though, is likely to vary with programme level and might in some circumstances be noticeable.

● *Telcom c4*. This is a sort of combination of dbx and Dolby A. It can give about 15 dB of noise reduction and does not need accurate line-up. It is relatively expensive.

134

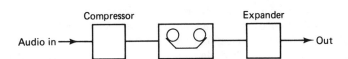

A simple companding system

	Dolby A frequency band	Possible noise source
I	Up to 80 Hz	Hum from 50 or 60 Hz mains
II	80 Hz to 3 kHz	Interference (cross-talk) from adjacent tape tracks
III	Above 3 kHz	Tape hiss
IV	Above 9 Khz	Tape hiss

Digital Audio

The microphone converts sound waves into fluctuating electrical signals (audio). In conventional analogue systems this continuous signal is amplified and processed. However, it easily becomes distorted, and degrades the resultant sound quality. In digital systems the audio signal is sampled at regular intervals and its strength at these points converted into numbers. These measurements are conveyed as digital information which is not readily distorted. Consequently, the final audio quality is similar to the original sound.

Digital processing

The analogue signal should be sampled at least 2.2 times the highest audio frequency to be handled. The most commonly used rate is 44.1 kHz. The amplitude of each sample is converted into a binary number, a series of BInary digiTs or 'bits' of information. The merit of this system is that it uses only two possible signal states represented by 1 or 0, sometimes referred to as 'on' or 'off' states, and the electrical signal is in the form of pulses. Consequently there can be marked degradation of this signal before it becomes impossible for a decoder to recognise the 1s and 0s. A digital system is therefore immune to the effects of interference, and it is possible to build in error detection and correction systems (see below). Thus digital recording is unaffected by tape hiss. Also, since pulses can be stored in solid-state devices, delay units, reverberation devices and other signal processing systems can be produced much more easily using a digital process than by analogue means.

Error detection and correction

In analogue systems it is almost impossible to correct satisfactorily any errors which may occur and affect the signal. In the digital domain, however, it is in principle relatively easy to detect and correct errors. The simplest method is known as 'Parity Checking'. In this the number of 1s in each digital 'word' is counted and made up to be an even number by adding a further 1 if necessary. A 0 is added if there is already an even number of 1s. At the receiving, replay or other decoding process, the number of 1s is again counted. If it is still an even number it is assumed that no errors have occurred. The presence of an odd number of 1s indicates that an error has crept in and steps are taken to reduce the effect. One such step is to repeat the immediately preceding sample, which, since these are only 1/44 000 second apart, will probably be inaudible. (Note that with this method of error detection the presence of *two* errors will be undetected. With a well-engineered system, though, the chances of this happening should be very small.)

More complex error detection systems, using several parity bits for each sample, can not only detect errors but can also provide a complete correction of the corrupted digits.

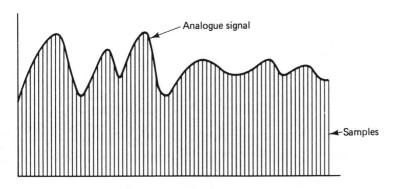

Analogue signal

Samples

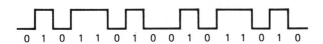

0 1 0 1 1 0 1 0 0 1 0 1 1 0 1 0

A 16-bit 'word' representing a sample.

The digital sampling process
The sampling frequency for high quality sound must be at least 30 kHz. 44.1 kHz is commonly used.

Signal-to-noise ratios
The weighted peak signal to peak noise, assuming the CCIR weighting characteristic is used and that no companding or bit-reduction systems are used, is given by:

$$6n-11 \text{ dB}$$

In table form this is:

No. of bits	Signal-to-noise ratio (dB)
10	49
11	55
12	61
13	67
14	73
15	79
16	85
17	91
18*	97

Note that there is a 6 dB increase in the signal-to-noise ratio for each extra bit.

* At present it is difficult to obtain this number of bits accurately and reliably.

Digital Tape Recording

Basic methods

The main problem is the wide bandwidth needed. Unlike the 20 kHz of analogue recording, a digital recorder has to cope with frequencies of the order of a few MHz. (This is because, taking a 16-bit system and a 44.1 kHz sampling rate, there have to be 16×44100 pulses/s. This works out at about 700000 pulses/s for one channel.) There are two general systems in use:

● *Stationary head machines.* A typical machine uses $\frac{1}{4}$ inch tape, thinner than conventional analogue tape and with special characteristics. The digital data are spread over several tracks, and can give the equivalent of the very high tape speed needed for the digital bandwidth. Such machines are very expensive at present. They have the advantage that tape can be edited with a razor blade, error correction systems taking care of the loss of data at the join.

● *Rotary head machines.* These are generally referred to as DAT (Digital Audio Tape) or sometimes R-DAT (Rotary head, Digital Audio Tape). They are in effect small-scale versions of video tape machines, the high tape-to-head speed being achieved by scanning the slow-moving tape with a fast rotating head block which is angled so that a series of slant tracks is recorded on the tape.

The cassettes used are small, $73 \times 54 \times 10.5$ mm, and the tape speed is normally 8.15 mm/s. The head drum has a diameter of 30 mm and it rotates at 2000 rev/min (1000 rev/min in certain modes). A playing time of 2 hours (3 hours with slightly reduced quality) makes the DAT system a very useful recording method. One may add to this the fact that excellent quality recordings can be made on machines which, in some cases, are virtually pocket-sized, and are of relatively low cost.

Editing

Very accurate editing is possible with DAT tapes but advanced technology is needed to achieve it. There are several systems available, of rather lower cost than was the case when they were first developed. Typically, sections of the DAT recording are transferred to a hard disc system combined with a large random access memory (RAM), from which access can be very rapid. Each section of recording thus transferred carries timing information (Time Code) and reassembly is performed in an almost automatic manner, the operator deciding on where edits are to be made. To aid the operator a screen display includes a simulation of an equivalent conventional tape movement, so that it is easy to see what tracks are approaching the mythical 'replay head'.

Front of typical portable DAT machine

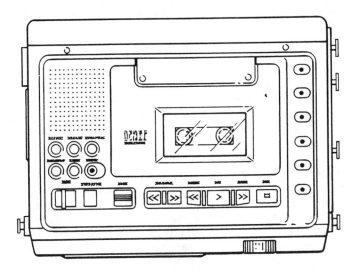

Top of typical small DAT machine

Compact Discs

One of the most important developments in sound reproduction in recent years has been the Compact Disc (CD). The original audio signal is converted into digital signals (see page 136) at a sampling rate of 44.1 kHz and using a 16-bit system. A version of these digital pulses is impressed on to a master disc using a laser. The latter produces a spiral track of indentations ('pits') in the surface. The regions between the pits are called 'lands'. Moulds of the master are used to make the replay copies in a way that is not unlike the process used with vinyl discs.

Unlike a conventional vinyl record the spiral track on a CD starts at the centre and works outwards. The density of 'information' is very great: up to about 75 minutes of stereo sound can be recorded on a CD. To achieve this the spacing between the tracks is only 1.6 μm (1.6 × 10^{-3} mm). This works out at over 6000 tracks per centimetre.

The linear speed of record (or replay) is 1.25 m/s. This is constant throughout the disc, unlike a vinyl disc where the tracking speed is greatest at the outside and slowest on the inside. This means that the speed of rotation of a CD must vary from around 500 rev/min at the centre to about 200 rev/min at the outside.

In replay a small laser is used with a complex optical system so that the difference between pits and lands is detected in the reflection of the laser beam from the disc. Accurate tracking is achieved by splitting the laser beam into three separate beams. One is used to read data, the other two being projected on to either side of the track. A greater signal from the reflection of one compared with the other means that the laser is going to that side of the track and a servo system moves the laser until the outputs from the two side beams are equal again.

Error correction

With such close spacing of tracks and tight packing of information a CD is basically very susceptible to errors. The tiniest blemish could cause the loss of vast numbers of digits. To overcome this, complex error correction systems are used. To begin with, the digital data (the samples) are scattered following a particular code. The same code is used to re-assemble the data correctly on replay. Thus a flaw on the disc is, in effect, distributed over a large number of samples and further error correction processes on each sample can eliminate the effects of the flaw. In theory a hole 1–2 mm across in a CD should have no audible effect. Some 25 to 30% of a CD's tracks is devoted to error correction!

Typical CD specification
Frequency response: 20 Hz to 20 kHz±0.1 dB.
Signal-to-noise ratio: 100 dB.
Harmonic distortion: less than 0.005%.
Channel separation: better than 90 dB.

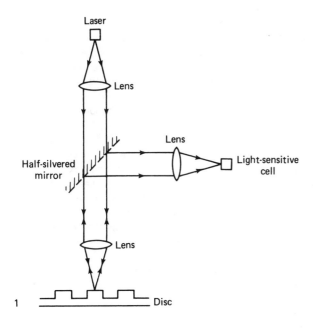

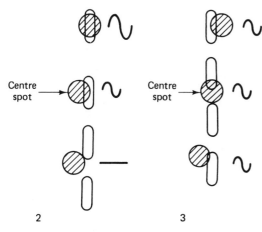

CD player
1. Simplified optical system.
2. Mistracking.
3. Correct tracking.

Sound Perspective

The term sound perspective means the apparent distance of a sound, as judged by the ears. A number of factors are involved but the most important is the ratio of the direct sound to the indirect sound. The direct sound is that which goes directly from source to microphone (or ear). The indirect sound is that which undergoes reflections first; it is in fact the reverberant sound.

In everyday life we are often unaware of sound perspectives, largely because, with two ears, it is possible for the brain to discriminate against what it regards as unimportant noises such as reverberation. However, a microphone system cannot do this, and consequently distances of a source of sound from the microphone often seem exaggerated when reproduced.

Matching sound and picture

Sometimes, but not always, it is important that visual perspectives and sound perspectives are in agreement. For example, in a dramatic context, we might have a dialogue between an actor near to camera with one seen to be some distance away. It will seem unnatural if the distant actor sounds as close as the near one. (It will be far worse if the perspectives are the other way round!) Thus we may need to have a close microphone on the near actor and a somewhat less close one on the distant actor. A degree of experimenting will soon show what is right for any situation.

There are many occasions when this matching of visual and sound perspectives is not needed. For example, in a commercial or a documentary, intelligibility of the presenters, however far away they look, is usually going to be much more important than the perspective of their voice.

Sound perspectives can be significant in music. The instruments seen at the back of a band or orchestra should normally sound less close than the front-line ones—and applause from an audience certainly should sound more distant than the band.

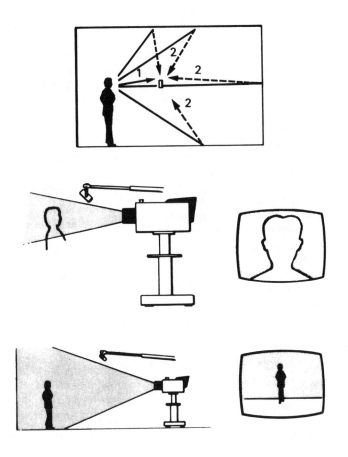

Direct and indirect sound
The microphone picks up a mixture of direct sound from the source (1), and reflected sounds from its surroundings (2)—walls, floor, ceiling. The closer the microphone to the source, the greater the proportion of direct sound pick-up.

Close ups
A close microphone position is required to give a sound perspective suitable for close shots.

Distant shots
For more distant shots, the microphone is positioned correspondingly farther away to provide an appropriate mixture of direct and reflected sounds.

143

Sound and Audience Participation

Programmes in which a studio audience actively participates (asking questions, contributing to discussions) present several sound coverage difficulties. A chairman, and any panel of speakers, can be covered by conventional methods such as microphones on table stands. It is the contributing audience that causes problems.

Broadly there are two versions of this kind of programme—that in which the members of the audience who are going to speak are selected in advance, together with the order in which they will speak, and the 'free-for-all' type of programme where the audience is largely spontaneous in its contributions.

Selected speakers

When the audience speakers are known in advance, one possible method is to have each person come up to a stand microphone, not forgetting that there must be microphones over the audience to pick up applause, laughter and similar reactions. With the stand microphone method good-quality pick-up can obviously be obtained but there is likely to be a slight interruption while a speaker leaves the seat to approach the microphone and the speaker is subjected to something of an ordeal. Consequently the 'naturalness' of the presentation may suffer.

If the audience speakers remain seated, an operator can hold a hand microphone in front of each speaker, particularly if the speakers are placed in easily accessible seats. (Note that if a radio microphone is used (page 116) it obviates the risk of awkward entanglements of cables with chairs and people.) Alternatively, a 'fishpole' (page 114) can be used.

Spontaneous contributions

Where audience contributions are spontaneous, the problems are greater. With a small suitably placed studio audience slung microphones can be effective in picking up comments. As a rough guide, in a non-reverberant studio one cardioid microphone can cover 12 to 15 people occupying a floor area of about 6 m². Thus an audience of 60 people could be covered by five or six microphones, provided the audience is reasonably concentrated. With this number of microphones it becomes necessary to have an auxiliary sound mixer on the studio floor. He/she can follow the action, and fade up only the one microphone needed for each speaker, the others remaining slightly faded down, so that comments from elsewhere will not be totally lost.

'Gun' microphones (page 112) can be used with good effect in this type of programme because an operator can point the 'gun' at each speaker.

144

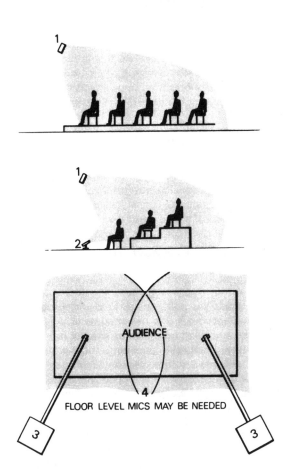

FLOOR LEVEL MICS MAY BE NEEDED

Floor audience
Where general sound is required from an audience seated at floor level, slung
microphones (1) may suffice (one microphone to about 15 people).

Tiered audience
Where an audience is seated at several levels (e.g. on rostra) slung microphones (1)
may need to be supplemented by a floor microphone (2) on a low stand.

Specific pick-up
Where specific individuals speak within an audience, two booms (3) may cover them
as shown here. Where the chairman indicates the next speaker the most suitable
boom has time to position itself. Spontaneous shots can result in delayed sound
pick-up.

Sound Effects Sources

At one time there were basically three ways of obtaining sound effects: (1) by actually creating the wanted noise, where this is feasible, in a studio; (2) recording on tape the effect and replaying it when needed (this was, and often still is, almost the only way of obtaining some effects); (3) using commercially available sound effects gramophone discs. The accurate 'cueing-in' of the last requires great skill.

In recent years, while all the above are still often important, the range of sources has extended. To add to the list, we have the following.

Compact Discs (CDs)
A wide variety of sound effects exists now on CD. Professional CD players can be set up to give very accurate, i.e. almost instantaneous, cueing of effects. If music is regarded as a form of sound effect then it should be noted that the CD is steadily replacing vinyl discs for music. Consequently (copyright problems having been solved) the use of music and/or effects in any programme will almost certainly need CDs.

Cassettes
Although we have made the point (page 132) that cassettes are generally inferior to reel-to-reel machines it is nevertheless true that modern cassette tapes, especially with a good noise reduction system, can be capable of more than adequate quality. Thus, this medium should not be ignored when considering replay systems. Small machines of high quality can be used for location recording of effects. Most are equipped with a noise reduction system. While cueing-up for replay is not as easy as with full-size tape, satisfactory results can often be obtained. The main drawback with cassette systems is that editing is virtually impossible, except by dubbing.

Cartridge machines
A cartridge machine ('cart' for short) is in some ways a specialised cassette system. Instead of the familiar compact cassette the cartridge is rather larger and contains an endless loop of tape running at, usually, $7\frac{1}{2}$ in/s (19 cm/s). It is possible to have up to about 10 minutes of playing time, although for jingles etc. much shorter tape durations are common: 30 seconds to a minute or so. The tape is drawn from the *centre* of the spool and returned to the outside, so that there is constant slipping between adjacent turns. This calls for specially lubricated tape.

The important feature of a 'cart' machine is that tone bursts can be laid to give an automatic cueing system, so that, for instance, at the end of the required effects sequence the tape is moved on to the start of the effect ready for another replay. (This is why relatively short tape durations are common. Spooling-on is relatively rapid.) With some cartridge machines more than one type of tone burst can be recorded to give tertiary cueing of other devices.

Digital machines using 3.5" computer disks with similar facilities are now common.

A modern cartridge machine

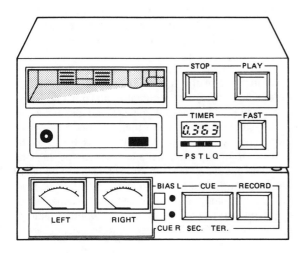

Typical performance specifications

1. CD player for effects reproduction ('cartridge CD')
   Display shows track number and remaining time.
   Frequency response: 20–20 kHz±0.5 dB.
   Signal-to-noise ratio: 92 dB.
   Start time on average: 200 ms.

2. Cassette machine (professional)
   Frequency response: 30 Hz to 20 kHz (+2, −3 dB).
   Signal-to-noise ratio, with Dolby C: 70 dB (weighted).
   Start time: almost instantaneous.
   Wow and flutter: ±0.1%.

3. Cartridge machine
   Frequency response; 40 Hz to 16 kHz, +1.0, −1.5 dB.
   Wow and flutter: less than 0.6% weighted.
   Speed accuracy: better than 0.1%.
   Start and stop time: less than 40 ms.
   Cue system: 1 kHz primary (automatic).
                 150 Hz secondary, user selectable.
                 8 kHz tertiary, user selectable.

147

Talkback in the Studio

Television relies for its success on the efforts of a coordinated team. Some are on the studio floor and require continual guidance and instruction, e.g. camera operators, others are located within the studio complex. To provide communication within the team an efficient talkback system is essential. This takes several forms: general, private-wire, switched and reverse talkback.

Production talkback
A microphone on the desk in front of the director relays his/her voice to camerapersons (through the camera cable), boom operators and other floor staff who wear headphones either plugged into wall sockets or radio receivers. The floor manager has to be extremely mobile and therefore normally wears an earpiece and microphone connected to a pocket transceiver tuned to the studio's radio talkback system. Adjoining technical areas (videotape, telecine etc.) are equipped with talkback loudspeakers. Where talkback is to be heard outside the studio complex, e.g. in the control room at an outside broadcast (a remote), a sound-line (control-line) is used to feed a loudspeaker or headsets. Some modern systems can use the vision circuit (whether radio or line) to multiplex or combine additional audio signals onto the vision signal, thus saving lines costs.

Talkback variations
Key-operated microphones enable the technical director, sound mixer and lighting director to talk on production talkback when necessary. A further key enables technical and production control room staff to speak on the studio foldback loudspeaker, should this be necessary. When used, the control room loudspeaker and normal foldback sound are cut to prevent howl-round. The facility is made inoperative in transmission conditions to prevent accidents.

For certain types of production, e.g. news, sport and actuality, the presenter wears an earpiece fed with switched talkback which can be operated by a switch in front of the director. This facility enables the director to pass instructions to the presenter even when the programme is 'on air'.

Private-wire intercom
In addition to production or general talkback various private-wire systems provide inter-specialist communication. The sound mixer requires independent talkback to his studio assistants and the boom operators need to be able to converse with the sound mixer (boom reverse talkback). Similarly, the lighting director requires an independent talkback system to communicate with floor staff (see page 150). In addition, various specialist control points e.g. the sound mixer and vision control/lighting have microphone/loudspeaker inter-communication panels and talkback to the director.

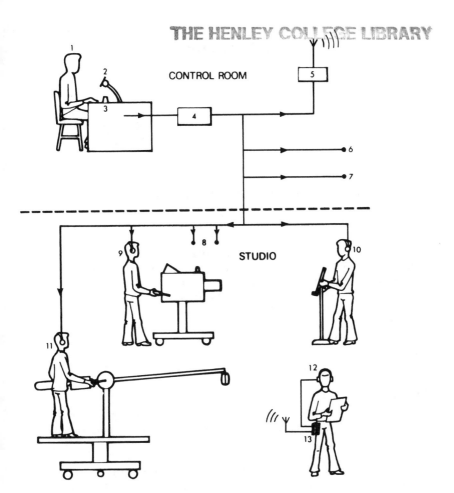

Basic studio talkback systems

A simplified illustration of the distribution of production talkback is shown. In addition private-wire switched intercom circuits exist between members of the team.

1. Director.
2. Director's microphone.
3. Microphone on/off switch.
4. Amplifiers.
5. Talkback transmitter and aerial for radio talkback to floor manager.
6. Talkback distribution to other destinations in the studio complex, e.g. make-up service room and videotape and telecine areas.
7. Talkback distribution to destinations outside the studio complex, e.g. outside broadcasts.
8. Distribution to studio personnel requiring talkback other than those illustrated, e.g. prompter operator and camera mobile crane operators.
9. Cameraman.
10. Caption operator.
11. Boom operator.
12. Floor manager.
13. Floor manager's receiver and aerial.

149

Communication in the Studio Complex

The principal means of communication within the studio is by production talkback (page 148). This, as we have seen, is also made available to recording channels and programme contributors (e.g. telecines or outside broadcasts) outside the immediate studio area.

Signalling

Comprehensive though the talkback system may be, it can become, if used to excess, a distracting background babel that either creates confusion and slows down the pace of rehearsals or is disregarded as 'intended for the other guy'. Directors can help matters by phrasing most questions so that they require only a straightforward 'yes' or 'no' answer. The cameraman can reply by rapidly tilting his camera up or down to answer 'yes' or panning right to left to answer 'no'. Rapid zooming in and out, or waving the camera around, shows that the cameraman is trying to draw the director's attention to his problem shot. Where there is a need to speak to the director he will do so over his reverse talkback circuit to the production control room desk. By the same token, telecine and videotape operators do not usually need to talk to the director. They have a button which operates a buzzer in the control room. One buzz in reply means 'yes' and two buzzes mean 'no'.

Intercom

In addition to normal talkback it is useful to have a 'keyed' intercom to enable all the technical areas to communicate with each other on a one-to-one basis.

Lighting intercom

While in the studio adjusting lamps, the lighting director needs to retain communication with the rest of his team (vision staff, electricians). Telephones around the studio walls provide private wires to key points (lighting console, etc.), but unquestionably the most effective method is a small two-way radio transceiver. This can considerably reduce the time taken for establishing communication between studio floor and control room.

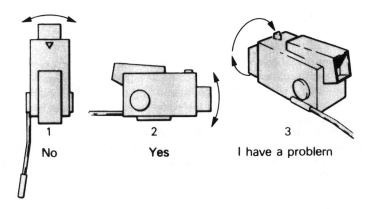

1	2	3
No	Yes	I have a problem

The cameraman's signals

The cameraman can reply to talkback questions and convey simple messages by camera movement. He can shake the camera head for 'NO' (1), nod it for 'YES' (2). A circular movement (or zoom jerks) means 'I HAVE A PROBLEM' (3). Rapid in/out focusing shows that he cannot focus sharply on his subject(s) due to limited depth of field.

Floor manager's signals

Signals from the floor manager can provide a range of silent cues and instructions to guide performers and audience. Typical gestures include:
cue (4); wind up within previously agreed time (5); cut finish immediately (6); move downstage (7); move upstage (8); you are off camera—go to next position (9).

Telecine

Telecine machines convert film into a television signal. One type uses a special projector to focus the film image onto three CCD sensors. Another, the flying spot telecine, uses a small TV tube scanned with a very bright raster. Light is transmitted through the film and an ingenious lens system on to photo-electric cells.

Since the industry has moved towards video acquisition for most applications, few small operators invest in a telecine machine because of the expense and low utilisation. For occasional needs facility houses offer a good service for film transfers.

Film gauge
The film gauge most widely used in television is 16 mm but its application is generally limited to documentaries where film is more appropriate for reasons of high humidity or extreme cold or for drama where the film 'look' still appeals. Recently, super 16 has become available providing higher resolution at a small extra cost. Where the highest quality is demanded and cost is less of a factor, for instance in commercials and the occasional prestigious drama, 35 mm film may be used. All professional film has the sound transferred from the original recording to a separate film covered with a magnetic coating. The picture and the separate soundtrack must be synchronised together prior to editing. Some old feature films have an optical soundtrack married to the picture as a stripe along the edge of the film and some old news material has sound as a magnetic strip alongside the picture.

Film leader
Film sequences are usually preceded by a leader which protects the film and enables an exact run-up time to be predicted. The leader is a standard length of film printed with countdown numbers in feet or seconds to the first picture. Some machines will run from a still frame or at variable speeds, others require a few seconds to achieve stable sound and pictures.

Colour correction
While the film is running, the operator compensates for and can memorise variations in density, contrast and colour using an electronic colour grader. This provides control of the exposure of the film and the characteristics of each primary colour to produce the correct colour balance over the whole tonal range.

The future
Whilst film has declined in use with the increase in electronic production, predictions about its demise have always proved wrong. It is likely to remain for a considerable time for the above applications and could even increase with the advent of high-definition television as flying spot telecines are capable of the highest quality reproduction.

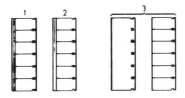

Film types
The sound recording associated with the picture on some historic films may be printed as an optical image alongside the shots (1), or recorded magnetically on a strip along the film edge (2). On modern films the sound is recorded on a separate magnetic film run synchronously with the mute picture (3).

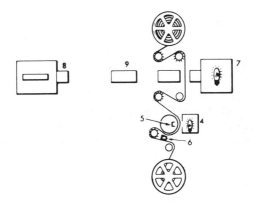

Basic CCD telecine
To reproduce a combined optical (comopt) sound track, a light beam from an exciter lamp (4) is projected through a fine slit onto the track, which fluctuates in density or area. A photocell (5) converts the varying light into audio signals. A magnetic sound head (6) reproduces a combined magnetic (commag) track. On 16 mm film the sound is 26 frames ahead of the picture from comopt, and 28 frames ahead from commag tracks. The picture is transported through a projector (7), and the image focused through a lens (9) into a camera (8). A synchronised transport ('mag bay') is used for separate sound tracks.

153

The Videotape Facility

Studio-based

The use and location of videotape recorders (VTRs) in a studio environment will vary according to the size and type of production facility. In a small set-up it may be preferable to have the videotape machines actually in the production control area or at least in an adjacent room, remotely operated by the vision control staff. However, this means that any post-production using these machines has to be carried out when the studio area is not in use.

In a larger installation or if greater flexibility is required, a separate VT area should be installed, with a central routing position. Machines can then be set up in pairs and editing and recording with two machines is easily achieved.

As videotape is relatively cheap, a good discipline is always to record studio productions on two machines; then if any tape fault manifests itself, a second master is available. The chance of both recordings being faulty at the same place is remote. This procedure can save considerable time, money and heartache, as well as providing a second master for three-machine editing (page 160).

On location

On location there are several ways of recording video

● With combined camera/recorders a set-up almost identical to that of a traditional film unit is possible. It is always worthwhile having access to a portable field player in order to check recordings before leaving the location, thereby saving time and money should a re-shoot be necessary.

● When using a mobile control room it is often convenient and operationally desirable to include a pair of videotape recorders alongside the vision control position. These can be operated by the vision engineer/lighting director in addition to their normal function. Complete programmes, if shot in sequence, can be simply edited on site using these two machines.

Tape storage

Videotape should be stored upright, in a dry, dust-free environment where the temperature and humidity remain low and constant. It is important that a suitable area is set aside as a videotape library.

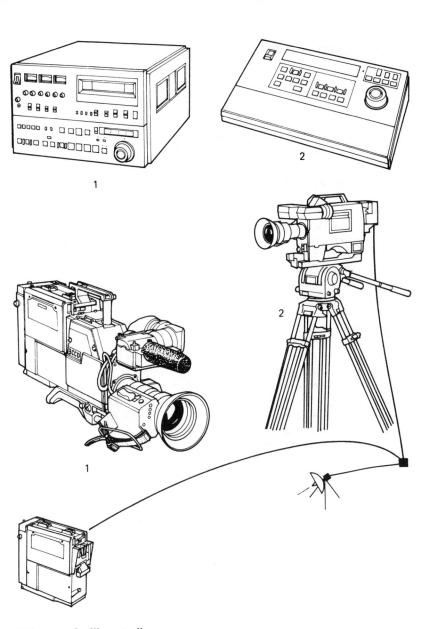

Videotape facility: studio
Videocassette recorder/player (1) may be in a self-contained VT area (which can also be used as an edit suite), or may be controlled remotely (2) from the production gallery.

Videotape facility: location
1. Camcorder (combined CCD camera and VTR).
2. Video camera (tube type) linked with portable video recorder or (either directly or via microwave link) with recording vehicle.

155

Videotape Recorders

A video signal consists of changes of information which occur at rates between 50 times and 5.5 million times a second! If the magnetic tape is not moving sufficiently fast, there will be insufficient room to record details of the video signal. Fast tape motion poses problems, and uses a lot of tape. So instead, the record/replay head itself is made to pass rapidly over a slow-moving tape, effectively producing a high recording speed. The result is a series of parallel slanting tracks across the tape.

Cassette VTRs

Open-reel videotape recorders (VTRs) have been superseded by a variety of cassette-based formats most of which are incompatible with one another. The professional formats are as follows:

● U-matic High Band, a now largely obsolete system using 3/4-inch wide tape.

● Betacam SP, a high quality analogue system using 1/2-inch wide metal tape.

● MII, a high-quality analogue system using 1/2-inch wide metal tape, but contained in a different sized cassette from Betacam SP.

● D1, a digital component system using 3/4-inch tape. This format is being superseded by other digital formats

● D2, a digital composite system using 3/4-inch tape. Obsolescent.

● D3 or DX, a composite digital system using 1/2-inch wide tape.

● D5, a component linear digital system using 1/2-inch wide tape.

● Digital Betacam, a component data compressed system using 1/2-inch wide tape. Digital Betacam machines can replay tapes recorded with an analogue Betacam SP machine.

By recording a signal in a digital form, *very* robust 'transparent' recordings are made, i.e. the replayed signal is *identical* to the original signal. When choosing which type of VTR to purchase, consideration should be given to budgets and applications, but beware: cheaper machines do not produce robust recordings. Picture quality degrades markedly from one 'generation' of recording to the next. If much editing/post-production is likely, then it is better to invest in higher-quality machines.

Typical idealised helical scan VTR format

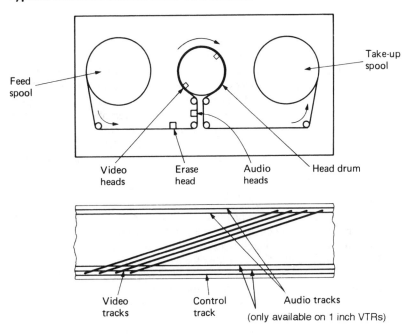

Feed spool

Take-up spool

Video heads

Erase head

Audio heads

Head drum

Video tracks

Control track

Audio tracks
(only available on 1 inch VTRs)

Tape formats

Type	Suitability
VHS	Domestic
S-VHS	Corporate/industrial/domestic
Betamax	Obsolete
Hi-8	Corporate/industrial/domestic
Standard U-matic	Obsolete
Low band U-matic	Becoming obsolete
High band U-matic SP	Broadcast/becoming obsolete
1-inch C format	Broadcast/becoming obsolete
Betacam	Broadcast/becoming obsolete
Betacam SP	Broadcast
MII	Broadcast
D1 -digital	Broadcast/becoming obsolete
D2 -digital	Broadcast/becoming obsolete
D3 (DX) -digital	Broadcast
D5 -digital	Broadcast
Digital Betacam	Broadcast
2-inch Quadraplex	Obsolete

Basic Operational Requirements of VTR

Videotape recorders need precise alignment to ensure consistent results. Test signals of known level should therefore be recorded at the beginning of every tape. On replay these signals can be used to check the replay systems to ensure that the videotape process is a 'unity' system, i.e. the original recorded signal and replay signal are identical. Colour bars are used for this purpose, derived from a test signal generator in the studio complex or when using lightweight cameras, from the camera's own 'bars' generator. Line-up tone is used in a similar way to ensure consistency of audio levels. It is generated within a sound-mixing console or from a lightweight camcorder's own line-up tone generator.

Idents

Some form of identification is needed for video when recording 'takes' or for complete programme tapes. It is normal practice to use a clock for this. Not only tape numbers, programme titles, detail etc. but counts into programmes are derived from this clock. It performs the same functions as a film leader on telecine. It can be generated electronically, or from a clock placed physically in front of a camera. It is worth noting that for location recording a film-type clapper board can be used. This gives the editor readily recognisable starts to, and information on, specific shots.

Pre-roll

Every VTR requires time for its mechanical and electronic systems to settle when it is made to play or record. This is known as *pre-roll*, especially when editing. Five seconds is the normal time, but this can be shortened to one or two seconds when playing into a studio. Beware of shorter pre-rolls if music is being reproduced as significant 'wow' occurs even though the pictures appear stable. About ten seconds are needed at editing, so ensure that at least this amount of stable material is recorded before calling 'Action'.

Timebase correctors

As VTRs are essentially mechanical devices, the video signal on replay does not conform to the standards of timing stability required by the electronics elsewhere within the television system. Picture sources need to be synchronous at vision mixers (page 76).

If a VTR is required to play synchronously through a vision mixer, a timebase corrector (TBC) must be used. This corrects the timing variation produced by the VTR. It is safe to say that the more this device costs the better will be its performance. Beware of cheap timebase correctors.

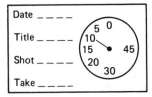

Videotape clock
It is good practice to identify your programmes or tape inserts with a clock (mechanical or electronically generated). It ensures accurate cueing and proper identification

Clapper board
Inherited from the film industry, the clapper board is as effective in identifying shots on location on video, except that the board need no longer be clapped.

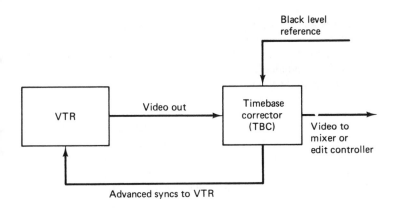

Synchronising the VTR
If a VTR output needs to be combined with other video sources, e.g. another VTR in an edit suite or a camera in a studio, a timebase corrector is required. The timebase corrector (TBC) needs to be referenced to local pulses and in turn provides an advanced reference to the VTR so that the video output arrives at the mixing point at exactly the right time. Professional machines have TBCs built into the machine. Non-broadcast VTRs need a separate TBC which may be more expensive than the VTR.

159

Videotape Editing

Initially the only way to edit tape was to cut it, but electronic means of editing have now been developed. These entail copying pictures and sound from one tape to another, called *dub editing*. Two types of editing exist:

● *Assemble editing*. This is the method of dubbing material from one tape onto a completely blank tape. The 'control track' (page 157) is 'assembled' along with the vision and sound tracks.

● *Insert editing*. This is where material is dubbed from one tape to another which has had a reference signal previously recorded along its entire length. This signal is normally black level with colour burst, plus the control track. The programme is 'inserted' over this reference. It should be noted that on many machines it is not possible to edit sound and vision separately in the 'assemble edit' mode. Therefore it is best always to record a reference onto the tape on which the programme is going to be constructed, before editing commences.

Three-machine dub editing

It must be remembered that a video recorder edits instananeously, i.e. goes into record during vertical blanking. Therefore, only vision cuts are possible. In order to achieve mixes, wipes etc. at least three machines must be employed: two play-in machines, one edit (record) machine and a vision mixer. Both play-in machines have to be timebase corrected to make them synchronous with the mixer. A shot or scene is laid down onto the edit machine from play VTR 1. When the vision effect is required VTR 2 is started and at the appropriate point the vision mixer is operated. The required effect is recorded onto the edit machine.

Some form of sophisticated machine control is obviously needed to make sure that the correct sequence of events takes place (page 162).

From the above the advantage can be seen of making two recordings at a time in studio. Copies can be made of tapes but quality is lost every time this is done.

When a vision effect is required each picture source making up the effect should be of the same quality for the best results to be obtained from the system. The original recording is called the first generation, a copy of it is called the second generation, and a copy of the second generation is the third generation, etc. The fewer the generations a recording has the better the quality produced.

As digital VTRs can be considered to be 'transparent', less care is needed to minimise the number of generations of recording during the editing process, when using these types of machine.

160

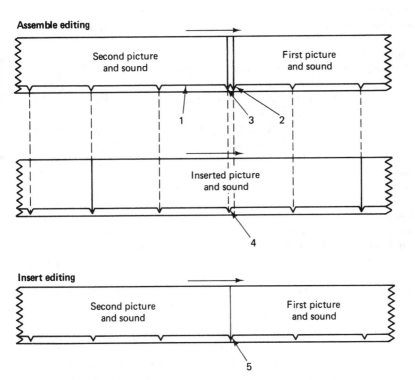

Assemble editing

Second picture
and sound

First picture
and sound

1

3

2

Inserted picture
and sound

4

Insert editing

Second picture
and sound

First picture
and sound

5

Videotape editing

With *assemble editing* the control track (1) is also replaced when the picture changes. Slight timing errors may lead to misplacement of the new control track (3) from the correct position (2). This disturbance may not be visible on a monitor but in any attempt at a re-edit a new picture across the join will almost certainly cause a picture disturbance at this junction (4).

With *insert editing* the control track remains undisturbed at the join (5). This control track has to be recorded prior to the edit session continuously from one end of the tape to the other.

161

VT Edit Systems

When a VT record machine edits, a sequence of events takes place that makes it change from play to record, in a special way. First the erase head(s) is/are turned on followed by the video and/or audio heads at *precisely* timed intervals. Electronic control is needed to ensure that this happens correctly, once the machine has reached its correct running speed.

Early editing VTRs only had manual editors, i.e. they edited when a button was pressed by an operator. Simple machines still use this method. It is inaccurate and cumbersome to do more than simply join sections of programmes together. True editing is not possible. The use of an edit controller which times the operation automatically may be one of two basic types.

Control track editing

Using accurate tape timers to control the edit sequence allows predetermined points to be marked, rehearsed, changed and performed relatively easily. This is a very common form of controlled editing. Microcomputers store both play and edit machine tape times. The computer 'pre-rolls' both machines for either 5 or 10 seconds (dependent upon preset switches), then runs them from pause, allowing the pre-programmed edit to take place.

These controllers usually operate with only two machines, and rely upon accurate reading of tape counters; these are prone to slippage, resulting in edits which are inaccurate by an order of a few frames.

Time-code editing

On an unused audiotrack or special track 'time of day' or 'elapsed time' information can be recorded along with the original programme. This is known as *time code* and gives the microcomputer a totally frame-accurate reference to use, instead of the tape counter. Time code is the key which unlocks the door to computer control of *all* functions required during post-production. Three or more machines can be controlled via a computer keyboard, vision effects can be triggered by the computer, edit details can be remembered on magnetic storage, lists made up from original edit sessions can be recalled and manipulated, and re-edits can be performed automatically. The problem of serial access of shots, i.e. removal of a sequence from the middle of a programme necessitating that all the following sequences need to be re-edited, is partially alleviated. 'Off-line' editing (rough cutting on cheap machines) becomes possible, loading data into the computer and then fine cutting 'on-line' using high-quality machines.

Time code is a series of pulses at audio frequency, used to indicate time of day or elapsed time. It requires a time-code generator when recording and a time-code reader when replaying the tape. Time code can be 'burnt in' on the picture and viewed without a separate reader on any television monitor—useful for reviewing takes and preparing editing schedules.

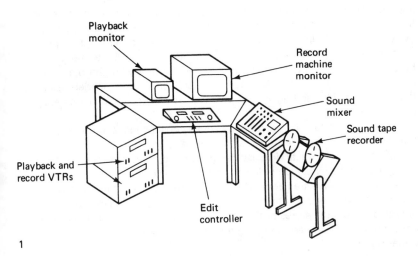

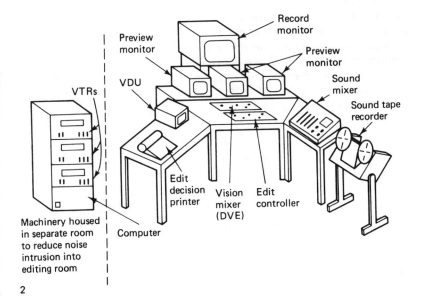

Videotape editing
1. Basic two-machine editing suite.
2. Typical three-machine editing suite.

Non-linear Editing Systems

One of the drawbacks of machine to machine editing is that the process has to be linear, i.e. it is only possible to edit a programme by adding one shot to another starting at the beginning of the programme and working through to the end in a serial manner. Changes to shots or sequences can only be made by copying the whole programme to another tape and performing the appropriate changes along the way. Traditional film editing has allowed sequences to be constructed, changed, moved and added to merely by undoing a taped join. The use of the 'trim bin' to store such sequences until needed has led to the belief that film editing can be more creative because changes are very easily made.

Methods of digital data processing allow a considerable amount of information to be stored in a relatively small memory. This memory is either solid state, magnetic or optical disk. By using standard computer techniques these memories can be read, manipulated and re-stored very easily.

Video pictures are transferred from tape into the computer store and then manipulated to produce a final programme. This programme may be transmitted directly from the stores or timecode information can automatically control conventional VTRs to edit the programme using original tapes in the conventional manner.

The control of non-linear edit systems is by means of a normal 'desk top' computer which displays video images and 'editing control' symbols. The editor selects the shot(s) required using a mouse, marks edit 'in' and 'out' points for both video and audio, the computer accesses the relevant memory area and stores the address of this memory in an edit list. By causing the computer to read out memory areas in different orders it is possible to readily and quickly change the way the programme is presented to the viewer. This process allows the video editor the same flexibility as that traditionally granted to the film editor.

Non-linear Editing System

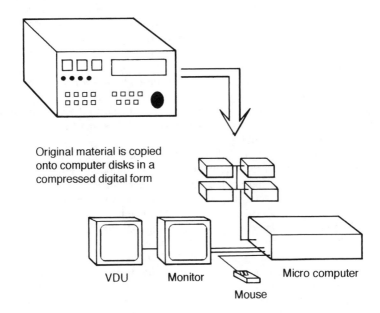

Original material is copied
onto computer disks in a
compressed digital form

VDU   Monitor   Micro computer

Mouse

Editing takes place in the computer's memory and an edit list is made up.
This list is used to perform an automatic edit using original video tapes.
It is also possible to transmit directly from the computer store.

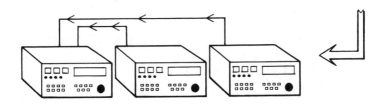

Post-production Suites

The arrangement of VTRS, edit controller, vision mixers, and any digital video effects devices in an editing suite is called a 'post-production suite'. Editing is a creative operation, and all control panels for ancillary equipment must be arranged so that the editor has immediate and easy access to them.

Equipment and layout

At the centre of the layout should be the *edit control panel*, with the *vision mixer/digital effects unit* immediately above or to one side of it. Within easy reach should be a vision monitor select panel, and to the right or left of all of this should be the sound mixing desk. (It is assumed that the editor also mixes and edits the sound.)

Assuming that the arrangement is for three machines (two play and one record), there need to be four small preview monitors, either colour or black and white, depending on the budget available. Each VTR has one monitor permanently connected to its output, with the fourth monitor connected to the output of the vision mixer/digital effects unit.

The *visual display unit* (VDU) is linked with the edit controller. It displays all the information relating to the editing process, i.e. in and out times, elapsed time etc. The position of the VDU will depend on the type of edit controller, but it should be sited such that it can be easily scanned by the editor, without much change in viewing angle from the preview monitors. A large colour monitor should be sited above and behind the bank of preview monitors. This should be selected to the output of the record machine under normal circumstances, but switchable to any of the sources.

Sound monitoring should be on two high-quality loudspeakers, one of which is always connected to the output of the record machine, and the other to the sound-desk monitoring circuit. An *audio recorder*, which can be remotely controlled by the edit system, should be placed within easy reach. This is needed to play sound effects, music, voice-overs etc., and to allow sound to be easily lifted from the VTRs to be used as an additional source for mixing and laying atmosphere.

Wherever possible all technical equipment, such as the VTRs, the editor, mixer/digital effects hardware etc., should be sited in a separate room from the control panels; the noise of cooling fans makes sound monitoring and indeed concentration over extended periods very difficult.

166

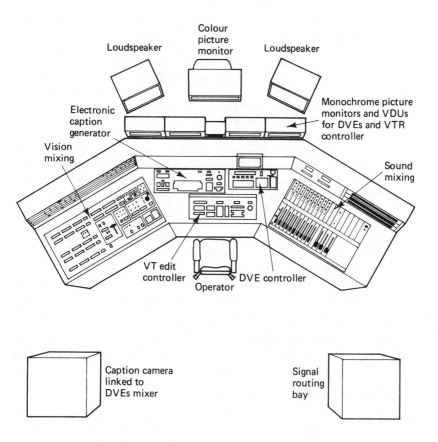

Loudspeaker

Colour picture monitor

Loudspeaker

Electronic caption generator

Monochrome picture monitors and VDUs for DVEs and VTR controller

Vision mixing

Sound mixing

VT edit controller

Operator

DVE controller

Caption camera linked to DVEs mixer

Signal routing bay

Post-production suite for video

167

Sound Dubbing

Because almost all television recordings are shot out of sequence, subsequent editing is needed and the final sound track must be largely put together as a post-production operation. Typically the studio dialogue is recorded on the videotape but music, sound effects and, where appropriate, narration are dubbed later. Note that only a limited amount of dubbing can be carried out in the edit suite. This is partly because VTRs carry only a few sound tracks and some of these are 'hidden' (i.e. integral with the vision tracks) and so cannot be manipulated separately from the pictures. The sound tracks available on the most common formats are given below.

The best way of producing anything other than the simplest sound track is to have a multi-track recorder which has 8 or 16 tracks, or possibly even more. The studio dialogue is dubbed on to one track (two for stereo) while a further track is dedicated to a time code, which means that with a suitable synchroniser the multi-track machine can be kept in step with the video signal on a separate machine. It is usual to put the time-code signals on one of the outside tracks, say track 8 or track 16, depending on the machine, and to leave track 7 (or 15) blank. This procedure eliminates any risk of the time-code signal being picked up by crosstalk on one of the audio tracks.

When the studio dialogue is transferred to the multi-track tape a copy of the video signals is made on a separate VTR. This can be relatively low quality as it is only used as a guide when the sound tracks are prepared. It is, of course, essential that both the multi-track sound tape and the new videotape both carry time code.

The dubbing process may be carried out in an area away from the main studio. Besides a multi-track audio machine, a replay VTR and synchronising facilities, there should also be additional tape and disc (including CD) replay facilities and a sound studio for narration and the creation of extra sound effects. A sound mixing desk is therefore also a necessity.

Sound effects, music, etc. can be very precisely matched to the pictures using this kind of set-up, as effects can be rehearsed against the synchronised VTR and, when appropriate, they can be laid on to the spare tracks of the multi-track machine.

Finally, the mixed sound track is relaid back on the master videotape, again running in synchronism.

Sound tracks on various formats

'Linear' means that the sound track runs parallel with the edge of the tape; 'hidden' means integral with the vision tracks; 'digital' means track digitally encoded.

- Beta—Two linear analogue, two hidden or two digital and two hidden.
- MII—As Beta
- D 1,2,3,5—Four Digital

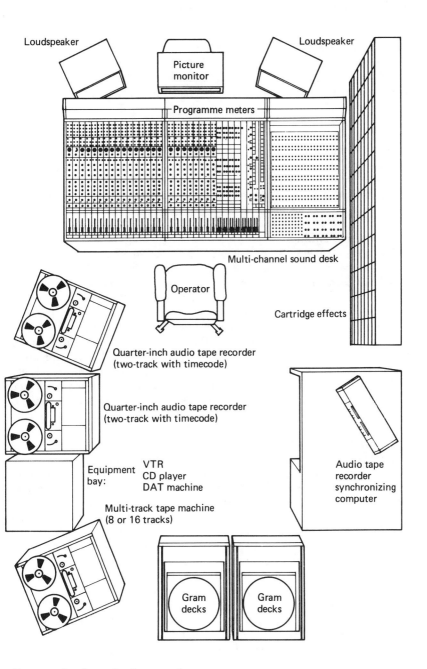

Loudspeaker

Loudspeaker

Picture monitor

Programme meters

Multi-channel sound desk

Operator

Cartridge effects

Quarter-inch audio tape recorder
(two-track with timecode)

Quarter-inch audio tape recorder
(two-track with timecode)

Equipment bay:
VTR
CD player
DAT machine

Multi-track tape machine
(8 or 16 tracks)

Audio tape recorder synchronizing computer

Gram decks

Gram decks

Post-production suite for sound

169

Programme and Production Planning

In the smallest installations planning is often on an ad hoc basis, but as the studio centre acquires more facilities (and staff) advance planning and scheduling of staff and facilities is required. Planning takes two distinct forms: overall resource management and the planning of individual productions.

Resource management

This coordinates the projected programmes and broadly estimates the staff, facilities and the financial commitment in adopting a particular schedule. In a large station this can include projecting the likely demands upon staff and facilities with a view to spreading the work load to achieve maximum efficiency and cost effectiveness.

Production planning

Production planning is concerned with the mounting of individual programmes. This is the translation of a script into the staffing, equipment and facilities required to mount that programme. Production planning is initiated at a meeting between the director and his team, including those concerned with design, lighting, sound, costume and make-up. Earlier meetings between the designer and director would have resulted in draft design plans being available for this meeting. The director indicates his aims and the team discusses the requirements and logistics involved before organising their own particular contributions. The time scale varies with the complexity and nature of the production and further meetings may be necessary to seek further information, to minimise compromises and to seek to maximise studio productivity.

Floor plan

The floor plan is a scale plan of the studio with details of its facilities, usually to a scale of 1:50. This plan indicates the available staging area, squared in convenient units (half-metre or 600 mm squares are suitable); other markings indicate the positions of the overhead lighting grid. Once the design is agreed by the team, the designer initiates the construction process while the production director uses a copy of the plan for his detailed planning of the action and camera treatment. A protractor is a useful tool for the director to check the available shots from a particular camera position.

As well as the staging and details of the furnishing, cameras, sound booms and other operational equipment are subsequently marked on the plan. Lighting treatment, too, is based on this plan, showing the position of all the lamps and associated requirements. This 'lighting plot' is produced by the lighting director so that lamps may be rigged in advance of the rehearsals. The more complex the programme the more detailed planning has to be.

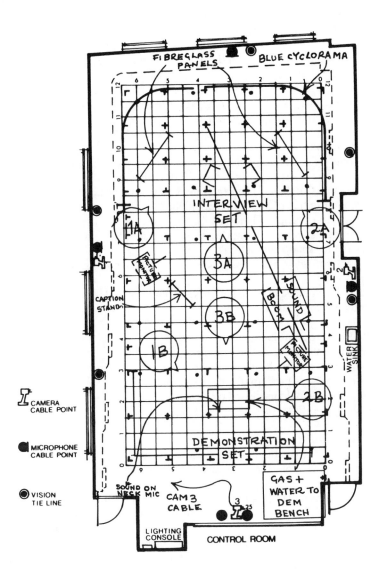

Studio floor plan

The studio floor plan shows the disposition of all technical facilities in the studio. Scenery is drawn on this plan, together with furniture. Subsequently camera and sound boom positions are indicated. Thus the plan serves as a valuable communications document. Cameras' positions shown as 1A, 1B, 2A, 2B, 3A, 3B.

Studio Discipline

Good studio discipline is necessary for the effective use of the studio, and the maintenance of good programme standards.

First, production discipline: it is essential that the programme is well planned. Don't wait until the studio day to sort out your ideas. Studio time is expensive! There must be one person in overall control of the studio operations—the director. All staff must keep to the timetable of studio operations, i.e. meal breaks, rehearsal periods, studio line-up recording time, etc. Good planning should result in few over-runs.

Avoiding disturbance
● There should be strict observance of the studio condition, i.e. on rehearsal, the need is for absolute quiet in the studio and minimum staff interruption in the control rooms. On transmission (and recording), the need is for absolute quiet and no interruption of any studio operations.
● Staff should be disciplined not to touch studio props, caption stands, sound mixing desks, vision mixing desks, lighting consoles, etc. which may have been carefully set up at rehearsals.
● Studio staff should avoid crossing the actors' eyeline—this can be very distracting.
● Visitors to the studio should be kept to a minimum, should keep quiet, and be permitted only under strict guidance.

Avoiding extraneous noise
● All studio staff should wear soft-soled shoes.
● All headphones not in use in the studio should be unplugged, to prevent inadvertent microphone pick-up of talkback sound.
● All studio doors should be closed properly.
● No talking in the studio (except actors).

General precautions
To ensure minimum frustrations to the engineering staff when they are lining up the camera, staff should avoid walking between the cameras and their line-up charts.

Access to fire exits must be kept clear. Fire lanes must be unobstructed.

There should be no smoking in the studio itself, except for the actors, if required to do so. At all times the studio should be kept as tidy as possible—no newspapers in the studio, old scripts disposed of properly, no cups/saucers on monitors, loudspeakers, boom platforms.

Equipment care
At the end of the production, time should be allocated for the proper derigging of equipment. Finally, remember the importance of allocating regular maintenance periods. Faulty equipment should be investigated and repaired as soon as possible—even if spare equipment is available.

Staffing and Responsibilities

Clearly, manning arrangements depend on the resource and its frequency of use. It is important to realise that a multiplicity of skills come together in the making of professional programmes and some training in all these skills is vital for the staff involved. In some applications the hire of freelance staff and/or facilities may be the solution.

Where a regular use of the facility is planned, dedicated engineering staff to look after and maintain the equipment are essential even though this can sometimes be minimised if it is possible to come to servicing agreements with manufacturers or servicing agencies. For operational staff, look for people with proper basic training as well as enthusiasm and creative ability. In small installations the concept of the operational engineer, a person who can combine engineering expertise with operational skills, is efficient and fulfilling but such people are quite rare. Flair and creativity are talents not easily acquired, but when coupled with training and experience, can produce the ideal member of a production team.

Small installations often employ staff with a range of skills rather than a single discipline but considerable attention to training is required to develop skills in a range of activities in which the person has an aptitude. Regular practice of those skills will also be required and attention to nurturing the skills can pay dividends in job satisfaction and cost effectiveness.

Staff members

Working on location with a single camera utilises fewer people but needs good rapport and the ability to work closely together as a team, sometimes for long periods in adverse conditions.

Studios are controlled environments generally working to a set pattern of hours. Productivity can be high but manning levels are also higher. The more complex installation requires more permanent engineering back-up for servicing and more operational staff. The Mobile Control Room (MCR) concept with several cameras is as labour-intensive as the studio.

Working on location whether with a single camera or with several cameras and an MCR may require a unit or production manager to sort out a multiplicity of problems such as permission, fees, parking, transport and hotels, depending on the scale of the production.

Another approach to manning is to employ key staff, hiring in additional people as required. This is often the most economic and efficient way of working for many small installations.

In some countries an awareness of trade union manning agreements might avoid possible difficulties.

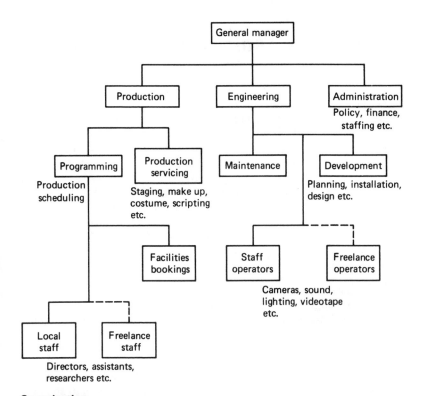

Organisation
The organisation of even the smallest studio complex requires the co-ordinated skills of many different professions. This organisational chart hints at the diversity that could be involved.

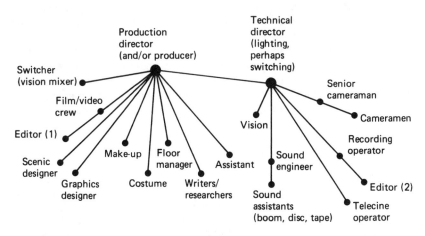

Production team
The Production Director co-ordinates the work of a team of specialists. Together they decide the artistic parameters of the show and organise the various services involved in production mechanics. Note: Editor (1) and Editor (2) may be same person.

175

On Location: Main Requirements

The key to successful location shooting is thorough planning, good discipline and the right equipment. The environment is usually not under control. The light, weather and extraneous noises from traffic etc. can play havoc with schedules and add considerably to technical difficulties. Non-broadcasters are more likely to use video rather than film on the grounds of ease of use and cost-effectiveness. Film still finds a place in prestigious productions and for certain special applications.

A location shoot carried out with the minimum of equipment to maximise portability is known as ENG (Electronic News Gathering). When more peripherals such as a monitor, remote control of exposure and colour balance of the camera, and a sophisticated camera mounting are added, the term often used is EFP (Electronic Field Production) or PSC (Portable Single Camera).

Camera and recorder
The choice of camera and recorder, sometimes combined in a camcorder or 'combi', is discussed on page 44. Suitable camera mountings are described on page 182.

Sound
The most stunning shots can be ruined by a soundtrack rendered inaudible by a passing jet or the local saw-mill! Locations must be chosen with sound as well as pictures in mind. The environment and the shots dictate the type of microphone to be used. To meet most needs a minimum microphone kit should comprise two personal (tie-clip) microphones and a rifle microphone, all equipped with wind shields. Some microphones require powering from batteries, so a small battery power supply or a small portable sound mixer is a desirable addition on all but limited ENG shoots. A battery-powered transmitter/receiver for radio control of any of the microphones can also prove useful. Use of the VTR for wild tracks (non-synchronised sound 'atmosphere') obviates the need for a sound tape recorder. A fishpole microphone support is a must. For portability and to reduce operator strain a folding carbon fibre pole fitted with an anti-vibration microphone stirrup is a good investment.

Lighting
Location lighting is discussed on page 178.

Batteries
Location equipment batteries are mostly of the 'nicad' (nickel-cadmium) type. Enough spare batteries should be taken on location for a shoot, though on-site charging is sometimes possible. Nicad batteries must be charged on the correct type of charger and life is preserved if used regularly and discharged fully before re-charging. A good charger will not only protect against over-charge but will also balance and 're-condition'.

Transit cases

All delicate equipment should be carried in lightweight transit cases lined with snug fitting shock-absorbing material. A checklist of contents on the inside of each lid is a good tip.

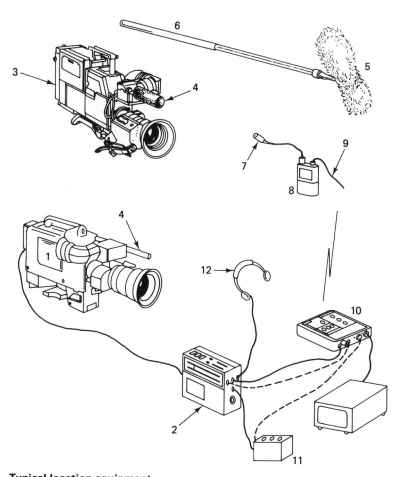

Typical location equipment

The camera (1) may be connected to a separate recorder (2) or they may be combined into a 'combi' (3). Whilst both systems often have integral microphones (4) these are unsatisfactory for most purposes. The most useful microphones on location are the 'gun' or 'rifle' microphone (5) on an extendable 'fishpole' (6), and the personal 'tie-clip' microphone (7) which may be connected directly into the recorder or through a miniature radio transmitter (8) that can be concealed about a person together with its aerial (9). The receiver (10) may be connected directly to the recorder or through a miniature sound mixer (11) for optimum quality control, especially if two or more microphones are to be mixed together. Headphones (12) are essential for good sound monitoring.

Do not forget your camera mounting (page 182), lights if needed (page 178) and, of course, spare batteries.

On Location: Lighting and Accessories

Portability and light weight are the key features of location equipment for use on simple shoots.

A recce of a location will indicate the level of lighting required. A kit of three or four small spotlights and one or two lightweight 2 kW spotlights, all with lightweight stands, would meet most needs. Large interiors may require additional lights to be hired, together with a generator if local power is inadequate or unavailable.

A battery-powered lamp can usefully fill dark corners or provide localised contrast control. HMI, MSR and CID lamps are discharge lamps with an approximately daylight colour temperature. They are high intensity sources but are expensive, discharge sources are usually hired unless frequently used.

Folding white reflectors or sheets of polystrene can be effective in reducing contrast by reflecting sunlight into shadows or softening the effect of hard lights. Large soft lights can be a useful alternative to diffused hard light, especially if there is a large area to light. Metal flaps (french flags) supported by brackets or stands in front of a lamp to take light off specific parts of the scene are sometimes useful. Important accessories include spring-loaded calipers (gaffer grips) for fixing lamps to convenient abutments, pipes etc., rolls of neutral filter (scrim) to soften the effect of the spotlights, and rolls of blue and half-blue filter to match the colour of the lights to daylight when working in mixed daylight and artificial light. Bulldog clips to attach the filter, mains extension leads, spare bulbs and fuses complete the lighting kit.

Monitor
A portable battery-powered monitor can be a major asset when lining up shots and for checking recordings, but it can be a time waster and battery guzzler unless used with care.

Clapper board and stopwatch
'Marking' a shot with a clapper board showing the shot and take numbers during the run-up time of the videotape machine is a useful aid to editing, though clapping the board is unnecessary as there are no synchronisation problems between sound and vision. A stopwatch for shot timing can also be useful.

Time-code generator
Most portable cameras generate time-code automatically, generally set to zero at the beginning of a shoot, although sometimes directors prefer to use the time of day.

Waterproof covers
All equipment liable to be exposed to the weather should have waterproof covers that do not impede operational controls.

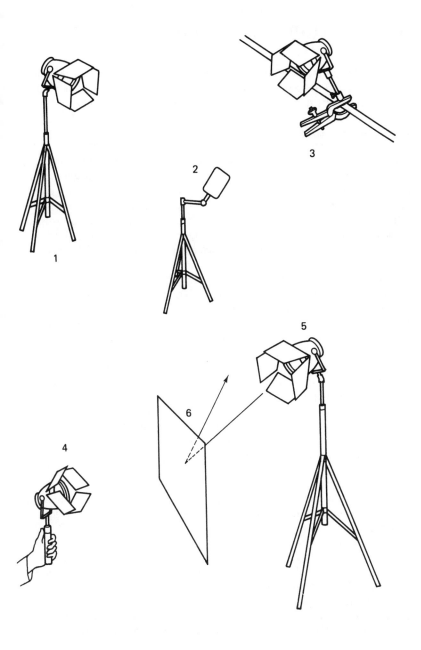

Typical location lighting equipment
(1) Small portable light on a stand. (2) French flag on stand to restrict area on which light falls. (3) Small spotlight clamped to an overhead pipe with a gaffer grip. (4) Small hand-held battery light. (5) Larger 2 kW spotlight with reflector (6) to soften effect of light.

On Location: Using Microphones

The type of microphone to use out-of-doors depends on whether the microphone is allowed to be in shot. It is usually perfectly acceptable in interviews for the microphone to be visible. In drama situations, most certainly not!

Microphone in shot

The two major problems are likely to be wind noise and handling noise. As a general rule omnidirectional microphones are less affected by handling noise than cardioids and they are usually less prone to the effects of wind on the diaphragm, although wind shields are almost certainly going to be needed unless winds are very light. For interviews a further advantage of an omni microphone is that there is no need for accurate pointing towards the speaker. Such a microphone held diaphragm upwards and roughly at chest height between interviewer and interviewee will normally be satisfactory.

Microphone out of shot

Here it is almost always necessary to use a highly directional microphone, i.e. some form of gun microphone with a windshield. There are some advantages in using the shorter type of gun with an approximately hypercardioid polar diagram, as, if mounted on a 'fishpole', it will be less heavy for the operator and will not need to be 'aimed' quite as accurately as a full-length gun. A suitable shock-proof mounting inside the windshield is essential.

For a solo presenter a miniature personal microphone can be used together with a radio-microphone kit. This arrangement can be quite inconspicuous and can give a good 'close balance' on the voice. Again, however, windshielding is necessary although the presenter's body and clothing may give enough protection on their own. Care will be needed in the positioning of the microphone to minimise rustle from clothing.

Monitoring out of doors

Almost invariably this has to be done on headphones, and even the sealed type which exclude a lot of external noise often do not give a very accurate version of what is being recorded, particularly in noisy environments. It is all too easy to make a recording only to find later that the amount of noise picked up from nearby traffic is totally unacceptable. With experience it becomes possible to allow for this sort of thing by putting some bass cut into the system. Sometimes it may be necessary to use correction at the post-production dubbing stage and here, a good range of equalisation equipment can be very useful in reducing the unwanted effects of extraneous noises without unduly affecting the voice quality of the presenter or actors.

Gun microphone
It is sometimes possible to mount a gun microphone on top of a camera (1) with satisfactory results, but there is a risk of the sound seeming 'too distant' in relation to the pictures. More usual is the fishpole-mounted gun microphone (2) fitted with a windshield.

181

On Location: Camera Mountings

Working on location poses special problems. Camera mountings need to be portable and robust yet still capable of smooth shot development. It is rare to find smooth tracking surfaces outside the studio. Thus some location mountings have pneumatic wheels to alleviate the problem and an adjustment to level the camera head when working on uneven ground.

Heavy cameras
A number of robust mountings are available for the heavier broadcast camera. They are generally lighter than their studio counterparts and are capable of being folded or broken down for transportation.

Lightweight cameras
These are sometimes erroneously referred to as hand-held cameras. They can certainly be hand-held but a professional cameraman would rarely do so unless for some compelling reason.

The workhorse mounting for location work is the lightweight tripod. It has pointed feet to sit firmly on rough surfaces, can be attached to a 'skid' (wheeled base) or 'spreader' (flat base) for smooth surfaces, e.g. a polished floor. The legs can be individually extended and the panning head levelled with the aid of a built-in spirit level. A good head will have an adjustment for correctly counterbalancing any camera over its whole tilt range and a friction adjustment for panning and tilting to facilitate smooth operation. A small tripod ('baby-legs') is also available for low-angle shots.

Sophisticated mountings
Lightweight portable pedestals are also available. Some separate into two sections (base and column) for transportation and have an ingenious method of utilising the column itself to pump air into the column to counterbalance the weight of the camera to enable smooth changes in camera elevation. For tracking shots it is often necessary to lay rails carefully levelled with chocks and to use a mounting that can be tracked on rails. A greater range of shots can be provided by a mounting fitted with a counterbalanced jib but this may need two or more operators. In tight spaces the 'hot-pod' (a uni-pole support) will assist the cameraman to hold a steady shot and the 'squatterpod' (a pan and tilt head mounted on a flat plate) is a useful table-top camera platform.

For the very ambitious, walking or running shots can be achieved by a very fit and strong cameraman fitted with a sophisticated harness, e.g. Steadicam or Panaglide, that gyroscopically isolates the camera from his jerky movements. Furthermore, mountings with longer jibs (for seated cameramen, and 'boom swingers'), anti-vibration helicopter mounts and even perches on hydraulic platforms (cherry pickers) may be hired.

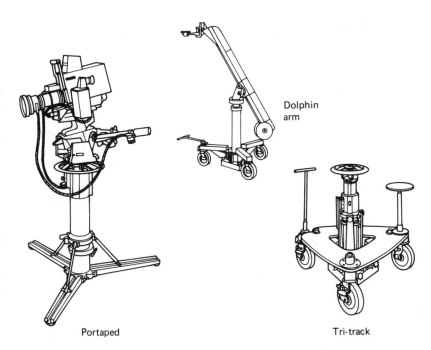

Dolphin arm

Portaped

Tri-track

The portaped

This versatile lightweight camera mounting has a pneumatic counterbalance for the camera and may be used in the studio as well as on location. The pedestal can be mounted on a skid (Tri-track) for simple tracks/crabs on or off shot, or the counterbalanced crane arm (Dolphin) can be fitted to the Portaped for more sophisticated camera movements.

The lightweight tripod

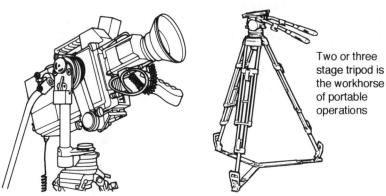

Two or three stage tripod is the workhorse of portable operations

The lightweight camera head

This type of head enables the camera to tilt about its own centre of gravity. It has an infinitely variable drag range and has a large tilt range. For ease of operation the viewfinder may be mounted on the head.

183

Further Reading

MILLERSON, GERALD:
The Technique of Television Production. (12th edn) 1990. Focal Press. London.
A comprehensive survey of the mechanics, art, methods and techniques used in television studio work. A practical reference work of encyclopaedic scope.

MILLERSON, GERALD:
The Technique of Lighting for Television and Motion Pictures (2nd edn) 1982, Focal Press, London.
A book offering a deep and comprehensive study of both the art and the technique of creative lighting for TV and motion pictures, from basic principles through the sophisticated and specialised applications.

MILLERSON, GERALD:
Video Camera Techniques. 1983, Focal Press, London.
A quick, lucid guide to the essentials of handling a video camera, both in the studio and outside.

NISBETT, ALEC:
The Technique of the Sound Studio. (4th edn) 1979. Focal Press, London.
An authoritative reference book for all who work with sound in television, radio, recording studio and film.

NISBETT, ALEC:
The Use of Microphones. (3rd edn) 1989. Focal Press, London.
A compact volume covering microphones and related equipment. Recommended for those primarily interested in sound balance.

TALBOT-SMITH, MICHAEL:
Broadcast Sound Technology. 1990. Butterworths, London.
A clear, easy-to-read explanation of the underlying principles of the audio equipment to be found in a modern studio.

WARD, PETER:
Basic Betacam Camera work. 1994. Focal Press, London.
A comprehensive handbook providing an excellent how-to-do-it guide. Written by an experienced practitioner.

WILKIE, BERNARD:
The Technique of Special Effects in Television. (2nd edn) 1989. Focal Press, London.
An interesting exploration into the world of television special effects.

Glossary

Acceptance angle Horizontal angle of view of a camera lens.

AGC See *Automatic gain control*.

Ambient General background noise level or basic illumination.

Amp (A) Ampere, unit of electrical current.

Amplitude modulation A method of transmitting information, by changing the amplitude (strength) of a high-frequency (carrier) wave in proportion to the amplitude of the lower-frequency signal we wish to transmit. The amplitude-modulated carrier is subsequently detected (demodulated) and the original lower-frequency signal recovered.

Analogue An electrical signal that is proportional to the originating source, usually pictures, sound or control signals.

Arc A largely obsolete powerful carbon-fed lamp.

Aspect ratio The ratio between the horizontal and vertical dimensions of the television picture frame. This is currently 4 : 3 for all television systems but new high-definition systems using 16 : 9 are likely to be the standard in the future.

Attenuator A resistance network introduced into a circuit, which enables the amplitude of a signal to be reduced without creating distortion.

Audio oscillator Apparatus which generates sinusoidal oscillations at frequencies in the audio waveband.

Aural sensitivity network A filter which 'has the characteristics of the human ear' (a precise definition has yet to be internationally agreed).

Autocue Trade name of a prompting device mounted on a camera so that the presenter can read the script whilst looking directly at the lens.

Automatic gain control (AGC) Device that reduces the dynamic range of an electrical signal.

B-format A one-inch broadcast recording system developed by Bosch-Fernseh.

Back projection (BP) Nearly obsolete method of projecting slides or film onto a translucent screen from the rear to provide a scenic background.

Backcloth (backdrop) A painted background, usually on canvas, to a set.

Background (BG) The part of a scene farthest from the point of interest, either vision or sound.

Background camera The camera providing the infilling picture that replaces the keying colour in *colour separation overlay*.

Backing (1) Background scenery. (2) A group of singers or instruments supporting the leading performers.

Backlight Light directed towards the camera from behind the subject, occasionally called *rim light* or *hair light*.

Baffle (1) A screen to deflect sound. (2) Louvred shutter for attaching to the front of luminaires.

Bandwidth The range of frequencies encompassed by an electronic system transmitting television pictures (video) or sound (audio) signals, the more detail required the higher the bandwith needed.

Barndoors Four flaps fitted to a spotlight which are used to control the shape of the light beam.

Barrel see *Lighting barrel*.

Betacam A combined camera and recorder.

Betacam SP A recording format widely used in broadcasting and elsewhere.

Betamax A domestic cassette format (obsolete).

Bias A high-frequency signal which is added to the audio signal in an analogue tape recorder.

Black burst Sync pulse signal that includes the colour burst used for synchronising picture sources, also known as **Colour Black**.

Black edge Facility for electronically creating a thin black edge around light overlaid lettering to improve legibility against backgrounds of similar tone.

Black level The lowest amplitude of a picture signal, representing black in a scene.

BNC The most common video connector used on equipment.

Boom A telescopic arm for positioning a microphone.

BP See *Back projection*.

Brace A strut to hold up scenery.

Brace weight An iron weight designed to hold a brace in position.

Brightness the amount of light emitted or reflected by a surface per unit area.

Bulk eraser Device designed to erase magnetic recordings.

BVU Near broadcast standard (or high band) U-matic ($\frac{3}{4}$-inch) cassette recorder, now almost confined to the non-broadcast market.

C-format Broadcast standard analogue system of video-recording using 1-inch wide tape now being superseded by digital formats.

C-mount A lens-fixing mount used on non-broadcast TV cameras.

Camera angle The horizontal angle of view of the camera lens.

Camera cable Cable connecting the camera to its control unit (CCU) or recorder.

Camera card Cue card showing a cameraman's own shots.

Camera channel Complete television camera chain including camera, control unit (CCU) and power supply.

Camera control unit (CCU) The device containing most of the control and line-up circuits of a camera that do not have to be in the camera itself.

Camera head See *pan and tilt head*.

Camera headlamps See *Headlamp*.

Camera left (Cam L) Left-hand side of the set from cameraman's point of view.

Camera mountings Camera supports including tripods, pedestals etc.

Camera right (Cam R) Right-hand side of the set from the cameraman's point of view.

Camera script Script marked up with shot numbers, cameras, cutting points, lighting and sound cues.

Camera tower Scaffold tower for high-angle shots.

Candela Unit of luminous intensity

Cans Accepted slang for headphones.

Capstan Main drive shaft for tape motion in a tape recorder.

Caption card Stiff card on which pictures or lettering are mounted usually black measuring 30 × 23 cm (12 × 9 in) or 50 × 38 cm (20 × 15 in).

Caption scanner Apparatus for televising 35 mm transparencies or small graphics.

Caption stand Stand on studio floor on which captions are placed.

Captions Photos, printed cards, other graphics and slides.

Cardioid microphone Microphone whose directivity pattern (polar diagram) is heart-shaped, resulting in maximum sensitivity at the front and very low sensitivity at the rear.

Cartridge A closed loop of tape or film in a near dust-proof container.

Cassette A near dust-proof enclosure containing reels of tape or film.

CCD Charge-coupled device, a light-sensitive material for converting light to electrical impulses.

CCU See *Camera control unit.*

Chalnicon A sensitive type of camera tube used in specialised applications.

Channel A general term for a succession of apparatus having a combined function. In a sound mixing desk, for example, a section handling the output of one audio source (e.g. microphone—amplifiers—fader—filtering, etc.) as opposed to a group of sources.

A *vision channel* embraces the complete video generating system for a single picture source (e.g. camera—amplifiers—associated supplies and scanning systems—switching circuits—distribution amplifier, etc.).

A *lighting channel* is the complete lighting circuit supplying a particular luminaire (e.g. power routing—switching—patching—dimmer—plugging, etc.).

Character generator Electronic generation of lettering or numbers for display on a TV screen using a form of keyboard.

Chroma key See *Colour separation overlay.*

Chrome dioxide tape A high coercivity, high remanence recording tape.

Chrominance The colour information in a video signal.

Cinemoid A proprietary branch of self-extinguishing colour gel used to tint light sources.

Clean feed An audio signal minus one or more of the contributing sources.

Clipper A video limiter.

Clipping level The threshold to which a clipper is set.

Clock A mechanical or electrical clock that counts down into a programme sequence or shot.

Clogging A partial loss of picture due to loosened tape particles causing a reduction in head-to-tape contact on a tape recorder.

Closed circuit Programme viewed but not transmitted.

Co-axial cable Cable consisting of an inner core and an outer screened braiding for carrying primarily video, UHF and VHF signals.

Coder Circuity for encoding the three separate red, green and blue components of a colour picture to produce a single composite signal. Whereas the original separate RGB signals required three individual transmission channels the encoded signal may be transmitted over a single line (cable or radio) and decoded to recover the separate components at the receiving point.

Coding (or encoding) The method of conveying colour information in a conventional television system, using a variety of techniques known as PAL. SECAM or NTSC. Other types of coding are used, for instance to combine digital audio sound with a vision signal over the same route or to combine teletext information with the video signal

Colour bars A test signal consisting of eight vertical coloured stripes.

Colour burst Several cycles of the colour sub-carrier transmitted at the beginning of each line in order to synchronise receivers to reproduce colours correctly.

Colour separation overlay (CSO) or chroma key The combination of the two pictures where one picture replaces a pre-determined colour in another picture (usually blue). In the latter case the desired part of the picture (the foreground) should not contain blue.

Colour synthesiser or matte generator A device for producing colours synthetically. Often used for colouring letters or backgrounds on black and white captions.

Colour temperature A scale for measuring the colour of a light source. Colour temperature is measured in *kelvins* (K), with $0°K = -273°C$. Tungsten lights are approximately 3200 kelvins, daylight around 5600 kelvins. The higher the figure, the more blue the light appears to the eye.

Composite video Signal containing vision and synchronising pulses.

Compression Control of audio sources to reduce their dynamic range.

Compressor Device to reduce the dynamic range of an audio signal.

Console A lighting or sound control desk.

Contrast The ratio of brightness in a scene.

Control line A telephone circuit between two areas for technical or production purposes.

Control track A signal recorded on a videotape to control the machine during replay.

Convergence the combining of Red, Green and Blue rasters on a colour monitor screen to obtain a single raster.

Convergence test chart A chart containing a grid of vertical and horizontal lines to enable adjustment of the images formed by the three primary colour sensors in the camera to be perfectly superimposed.

Coving A concave board at the front of a cyclorama to conceal the floor line.

Cox-box A proprietary make of colour synthesiser.

Crab To move a camera sideways.

Credits Programme titles or end titles.

Cross colour An interference pattern on fine detail such as a herringbone jacket.

Cross fade To mix from one source to another (vision, lighting or sound).

Crosstalk Interference between one source and another (vision or sound).

CRT Cathode ray tube.

Crushing Loss of gradation in a picture due to distortion of the contrast range of a camera.

CSO See *Colour separation overlay*.

Cue light A small light mounted on a floor or table stand in the studio that is switched on from the control room in order to cue an artist

Cue track Sub-standard audio track, used for cueing or guide purposes

Cut instantaneous change from one picture to another.

Cyc track A rail with runners on which a cyclorama is hung

Cycles per second See *Hertz*.

Cyclorama (cyc) A plain backcloth stretched taut around a studio to provide a backing.

dB Decibel, a logarithmic measure of sound intensity. Also used for comparing signal levels.

dBA A measure of sound levels in decibels weighted by the subjective effect on the human ear.

Decoder Circuitry for retrieving the individual Red, Green, Blue colour signals from a coded colour video signal.

Definition The ability to reproduce fine detail in a picture.

Defocus The blurring on an image optically or electrically.

Degausser Device for demagnetising tape heads or videotapes.

Depress To lower a camera height (on a pedestal mounting, by reducing the column height).

Depth of field The distance between the nearest and farthest points from a camera that are within acceptable focus. Depth of field varies with lens aperture (stop), focused distance, and the focal length of the lens.

Dichroic mirror A surface-coated glass filter which permits certain parts of the visible spectrum to pass through while reflecting others. Used in colour television cameras and telecine systems to analyse the full-colour scene into RGB components. A form of dichroic filter is used as a heat filter in projector systems to protect the film material from infra-red and heat rays.

Digital The representation of video, audio or control signals by means of a train of pulses.

Dimmer A device for control of lamp brightness.

Directivity pattern A graphical plot representing the relative performance of a device at different distances and in various directions. It can show the sensitivity variations, or changes in frequency response, of a microphone. Similarly it can demonstrate the way in which the output of a device (e.g. a lamp or a loudspeaker) alters with angle and with distance.

Director The person responsible for the organisation, creative interpretation and presentation of a particular programme. The functions of a director vary somewhat from one organisation to another.

Dissolve An effect of fading one picture out whilst another is faded in.

DNR Digital noise reduction.

Dolby Trade name for a particular type of noise reduction.

Dolly A wheeled camera mounting, usually larger than a pedestal or more suited to uneven surfaces.

Double band Separate pictures and sound tracks (known as Sepmag) shown on a film projector.

Double-head Film projection and sound on separate synchronised projectors.

Downstage The activity area nearest to the camera. To walk downstage means to walk towards the cameras.

Dropout Momentary break in the recording track on videotape causing a flash on one or more lines on the screen.

Drum The assembly containing the rotating heads on a videotape machine.

Dual source Light with a hard source at one end switchable to a soft source at the other.

Dubbing (1) Copying a recorded sequence or programme. (2) Audio manipulation of a recorded video sequence or programme.

Dynamic range Variation between the highest undistorted sound level from a device and the inherent background noise level. Similarly for video signals.

E to E Electronic to Electronics, i.e. a signal passing through a device but not acted upon by that device.

Echo Reverberation, often added artificially by means of electronic devices.

Edit suite An area containing two or more tape machines configured to join sequences together.

Editing Assembling a programme by joining separate sequences together in an ordered way.

Effects Sound or visual material added to a scene to create atmosphere.

Effects track Sound track of effects excluding dialogue and music.

EFP Electronic field production, using portable TV equipment. The programme requirements are technically more complex than news and current affairs.

Electret A permanently charged material used in some types of electrostatic microphone.

Electronic editing Videotape editing from one or more videotape machines to another, equipped to make invisible joins electronically.

Electrostatic microphone Microphone in which the conducting diaphragm upon which the sound impinges forms one plate of a capacitor. Capacitance changes caused by diaphragm movements are converted into an output voltage.

Elevate To raise camera height.

Encoding See *Coding*.

ENG Electronic news gathering, using videotape as the recording medium and generally lightweight equipment.

f-number Calibration of lens aperture, calculated by dividing the focal length by the effective iris-aperture diameter.

Fade To increase or decrease the amplitude of a picture or a sound, as in 'fade-up', 'fade-down', or fade-in, fade-out.

Fader Lever for fading sound, pictures or lights.

FAP or **FP** See *Front axial projection.*

Field One half of the interlaced television frame, one field consisting of all the odd lines in a picture the other the even lines.

Figure-of-eight Type of microphone directivity pattern (so called from its polar diagram shape). The true three-dimensional pattern would be two spheres in contact with the microphone at the point of contact.

Filler light Soft light that reduces the density of shadow in a picture.

Film recording Transfer of an electronic video signal to film.

Firelane, Lane marked on the studio floor to limit the acting area and leave a free passage between the set and the studio wall.

Fisheye lens An extremely wide angle lens.

Fishpole Hand-held microphone boom.

Flare Effect of a bright source of light shining directly onto a lens, sometimes done for effect but more often an undesired aberration.

Flat A flat piece of scenery usually made of stretched canvas or hardboard on a flat wooden framework. Sometimes with architectural features such as a door or window.

Flat light Even illumination of a scene, giving no modelling and a two-dimensional appearance.

Flood A soft source of light.

Floor lamp A light source on a stand.

Floor manager The person responsible for the productional organisation (including performer cueing) and general discipline in the studio. He is the director's representative on the floor.

Floor paint A paint used for studio floors that can be washed off, often used in conjunction with a patterned roller.

Floor plan Plan of a studio (usually to a scale of 1:50) showing the disposition of sets, furniture and equipment.

Flutter Rapid variation in speed of a recording medium.

Flying erase head A rotating video head used to erase video tracks when electronic editing on videotapes.

Flying spot scanner Device using a plain raster viewed by image sensors through film or slides to produce a picture free of registration error.

Focal length Distance from the optical centre of a lens to the point of focus of an object at infinity.

Foldback Sound fed to a loudspeaker on the studio floor from the sound mixer.

Frame Television picture comprising two fields.

Frame store (synchroniser) Device that can store an incoming signal and replay it in synchronism with a local reference, thus enabling remote pictures to be mixed with local pictures.

Frequency modulation (FM) A method of transmitting information by changing the frequency of a high-frequency carrier wave in proportion to the amplitude of the lower-frequency signal we wish to transmit. (The amplitude of the carrier remains unchanged.) The frequency-modulated carrier is subsequently demodulated to recover the original signal.

Fringing Colour errors at the edge of coloured areas in a picture.

Front axial projection (FAP) The projection of a background scene through a half-silvered mirror on to a highly reflective screen viewed on axis by a camera through the mirror. Now rarely used.

Gain Measure of amplification or attenuation, usually in decibels.

Gallery Production control room.

Genlock The control of the local pulse generator by a remote source to make pictures from both areas synchronous at the mixer.

Gobo Metal 'cut-out', used in projection of abstract shapes, clouds, windows, etc.

Grams Record playing equipment.

Grey scale Test card showing graded steps from black to white, used for line-up of colour cameras and colour monitors

Grille Test signal consisting of vertical and horizontal lines on a contrasting background.

Ground row (1) Floor lamps used to light a cyclorama or backcloth. (2) Scenic cut-outs, usually floor standing and of reduced height; can be used to hide lighting ground row.

Group In a sound desk two or more channels may be faded up together, and so combined into a group. A single group fader then controls all these sources simultaneously.

Guide track (1) Pre-recorded sound track used to synchronise action. (2) Sound track recorded during shooting to serve as a guide during post-synchronising, but not used in the main programme.

Gun microphone Type of microphone with a narrow pick-up angle. Such microphones embody a slotted or perforated tube, typically about 0.5 m long.

Gyroscopic errors Unstable recording due to a portable VTR being moved around during recording.

Hard light Luminaire that produces clearly defined shadows, e.g. a spotlight.

Harmonic An oscillatory motion (mechanical or electrical) that is a multiple of a fundamental frequency.

Harmonic distortion Changes in the total harmonic content in a signal caused by non-linear circuits.

Head Pan and tilt device supporting a camera.

Head clog Build-up of oxide particles from videotape on to the video head, causing a reduction or total loss of picture during recording or playback.

Head gap The magnetic gap between the poles in tape recorder heads.

Headlamp Luminaire mounted on a camera.

Headset Headphones, sometimes with microphone attached.

Helical scan Method of recording where videotape is wound in a helix around the drum carrying the video heads. Method used in all VCRs.

Hertz (Hz) Unit of frequency.

High band See *BVU*.

High energy tape Tape with higher coercivity than ferric oxide and giving improved picture quality.

High key High luminance pictures, generally with low colour saturation.

House lights Working lights in a studio.

Howl-round A whistling effect caused by sound from a loudspeaker being picked-up by a microphone which feeds the sound directly back to the loudspeaker again.

Illumination A measure of the amount of light incident on a surface. It is measured in lux (lumens/m²) or foot-candles (lumens/ft²).

Infill Picture source placed within a foreground shape in another picture. using *colour separation overlay*.

Inlay A picture keying itself into another picture so that the former becomes the foreground in the latter picture, e.g. name captions over studio pictures.

Iris The variable diaphragm that controls the amount of light passing through a lens.

Jack Type of audio socket consisting of concentric contacts separated by, insulators.

Jack field Multiple rows of jacks (may also apply to rows of video sockets).

Jack plug Audio plug with two or three concentric contacts.

Jelly Gelatine or plastic translucent material used to diffuse or colour a light source.

Kelvin See *Colour temperature*

Key light The primary light that establishes the shape or form of an object.

Keying colour The colour providing the switching signal in *colour separation overlay* or chroma key

Kilowatt (kW) One thousand watts.

Lantern Studio lighting unit or luminaire.

Lead oxide vidicon A camera tube more usually known as a 'plumbicon', now superseded by CCD sensors.

Leader Standard length of film or videotape at the front of a programme to ident the programme, protect the beginning of the programme from damage, and enable machinery to run up to the correct speed before the start of the programme.

LED Light-emitting diode.

Leddicon Trade name for a lead oxide vidicon.

Lens hood Device attached to the front of a lens to minimise the possibility of lens flares.

Lift An electronic adjustment in camera or telecine channel (usually operated continuously for optimum picture equality), which moves all picture tones up or down the tonal scale. This is achieved by adjusting the video signal's DC level relative to picture black level.

Light box An evenly illuminated ground glass screen, usually lit with fluorescent tubes. Used for viewing transparencies.

Lighting barrel Bar from which luminaries are suspended.

Lighting console Control unit for adjusting the brightness of individual lamps and memorising combinations of settings.

Lighting hoist Machinery for raising or lowering luminaires.

Lighting plot Plan of the lighting rig for a particular programme.

Lighting rig (1) An arrangement of luminaries for a particular programme. (2) The installed lighting in a studio, including luminaires, suspension and hoists.

Limiter Device for restricting the maximum amplitude of a vision or audio signal.

Line standard The number of lines making up the TV picture (625 in Europe, 525 in the USA and Japan).

Line-up (set-up) Check on the technical performance of equipment prior to broadcasting or recording.

Linear source A tungsten halogen strip light typically 119 mm long and 13 mm in diameter. Used in soft-light sources and cyc lights.

Lines (1) Scanning structure of a TV picture. (2) Circuit external to a centre booked through local BT operators. (3) Measure of the ability to resolve picture detail (a broadcast camera may have a resolution of 700 lines).

Lip mic Ribbon microphone used very close to the presenter's mouth to exclude external sounds in noisy environments.

Low-angle dolly Camera mounting that enables the camera lens to go very close to the ground.

Low band Standard U-matic (3/4 in) recording, non-broadcast quality.

Low key Picture where the majority of tones are low luminance.

Lumen Unit of luminous flux or quantity of light emitted per second.

Luminaire Lighting unit or lantern.

Luminance Brightness part or monochrome part of a colour picture.

Lux Metric unit of illumination. 1 Lux = 1 Lumen/m²

M-format An integrated broadcast quality camera/recorder system using the VHS cassette size but not compatible with standard VHS.

Master First generation recording.

Master tape Final edited version of a videotaped programme.

Matte A mask, electronic or physical, used to obscure one picture and replace with another of the same size, dimension and position as the mask.

Matte generator See *Colour synthesiser.*

Megahertz (MHz) One million *hertz.*

Mic Microphone.

Mix A transition between one picture and another where one picture fades out whilst the other fades in.

Mixer Equipment devised to select and mix sound or vision sources individually or combined at any desired level.

Modulator An electronic facility used when television signals are to be distributed by coaxial cable over an appreciable distance, or made available at a number of monitoring points throughout an area. By superimposing the picture and sound signals on a radio frequency carrier, high quality results are achievable, viewed on conventional TV receivers.

Moiré Fine pattern on the screen caused by interference between picture elements and subcarrier.

Monitor Video display screen.

Monochrome (mono) Picture without colour information.

Multiplex A system of coding signals so that more than one can be carried on a single cable or radio frequency carrier such that each individual signal can be decoded at the receiving end.

Munsell system A system of colour notation, classifying a wide range of hues at varying degrees of saturation. The luminance of a surface is scaled in values from 10 (White) to 0 (Black). Surfaces with the same luminance value will appear the same tone (shade of grey) on a monochrome display.

Musa Professional video connector used mainly on vision distribution equipment and *jack fields*.

Music circuit (programme line) A high-grade sound line permitting wide-band, low-distortion transmission of audio signals, particularly between a remote source and its destination.

Mute Film or videotape without sound.

Newvicon Camera tube of a vidicon type but more sensitive than a vidicon.

Nicad battery Nickel cadmium battery.

Noise (1) Random dots on a picture (snow). (2) Background hiss, hum, etc. on sound.

Non-composite Vision signal minus synchronising pulses.

Non-sync Vision signals not synchronised with each other.

North light Large soft light source.

NTSC (National Television Systems Committee) Colour television system used in the USA, Canada and Japan.

Overlay See *Colour separation overlay*.

Overscan The normal domestic display of a picture whereby some of the linage is lost at the edge of the screen.

PA (1) *Public address* system. (2) Production assistant (person who assists director).

Paint Box Electronic painting device using a tablet and electronic stylus manufactured by Quantel.

PAL (Phase alternate line) Colour television system used in most of the countries of Western Europe.

Pan Rotation of a camera through a horizontal arc, thus 'pan right' and 'pan left' (Note: sometimes used incorrectly for *tilt*, hence 'pan up' and 'pan down'.)

Panning head Device between camera and its mounting, enabling smooth panning and tilting of the camera.

Pantograph A spring-counterbalanced, collapsible, lighting suspension unit designed on the lazy-tongs principle. Units are available which allow the heights of luminaire of various weights to be adjusted easily over a wide range.

Passes Number of times a recorded videotape passed the video head to produce further recordings on a VT build-up.

Patch panel A system for connecting luminaires distributed about the studio with a selected series of supply circuits (usually incorporating dimmers/switching/protection devices). It frequently takes the form of a plug and socket (jackfield) arrangement.

PDA See *Pulse distribution amplifier*.

Peak programme meter (PPM) Device for indicating peaks of sound levels.

Peak white Maximum level of a vision signal.

Pedestal Single manned studio camera mounting enabling smooth shot development, including camera height.

Periscope Optical device for taking low-angle shots.

Perspective (sound) The illusion of distance of a sound source.

Perspective (vision) In pictorial terms, an illusion of depth and space created by the use of decor, lighting and lens-angle selection. It is essential for picture and sound to maintain related perspective to create a co-ordinated effect.

PFL See *Pre-fade listen*.

Phantom power DC power provided down the audio cable for electrostatic microphones.

Phase distortion Distortion arising when the relative phases of component parts of a complex wave are changed.

Playback (1) Replay of recorded material. (2) Replay of pre-recorded music for performers to sing or dance to.

Plumbicon Trade name for a lead oxide vidicon tube, now largely superseded by CCD sensors.

Portapak Battery-powered videotape machine.

Positioner Vision mixing facility for positioning wipes on the screen.

Post dub Recording of additional information on a sound track after the main recording has been completed.

Post-synchronise To attempt to add synchronised sound (e.g. dialogue or music) after the pictures have been shot.

PPM See *Peak programme meter*.

Pre-fade listen (PFL) Facility on sound mixers to enable sound sources to be checked before being faded up.

Pre-record Record part of a programme before the main recording.

Presence Boosting the mid-range frequencies (3–8 kHz) of an audio signal to improve subjective sound quality.

Preview (1) Advance showing of a programme. (2) Checking a picture before its use in a programme. (3) Band of switches on a vision mixer permitting advance selection of sources before putting them on transmission.

Producer The person responsible for the overall planning, financial control and artistic shape of a series of programmes.

Profile lamp Luminaire with focusing lens for projecting images on to a background.

Prop(s) Properties. Movable articles used for set dressing or as part of the action.

Public address (PA) In television studio operations, a feed of selected sources being reproduced by loudspeakers near a studio audience.

Pull focus Change the plane of focus in a scene to draw attention to a new point of interest.

Pulse distribution amplifier (PDA) Used for distributing the necessary pulses to camera and other vision equipment needing synchronisation.

Purity The correct rendition of a plain colour on a cathode ray tube.

QI Quartz iodine lamp. See *Quartz halogen*.

Quadruplex recorder Professional videotape machine using 2-inch wide tape and orthogonal scanning, now completely superseded by helical scan machines. Some specialist companies are able to transfer historic recordings on this format.

Quartz halogen Lamp made of quartz glass and filled with halogen gas, used in most modern studio lights.

Raster The bright rectangular area formed on the screen of a television picture tube (by an unmodulated scanning beam tracking an interlaced line pattern on its phosphor surface).

Registration The combining of Red, Green and Blue camera images to obtain a single image.

Reverberation The prolongation of sound caused by repeated reflections from walls, floor, ceiling etc.

Reverberation time The time taken for the reverberant sound to decay through 60 dB.

Reverse talkback Talkback from a destination to the source, e.g. cameraman to director.

RGB Primary colours (red, green, blue) of television system.

Rostrum (1) Raised platform in the studio. (2) Flat bench for stills, animations or model work.

Rostrum camera Camera supported over a flat bench with calibrated control of panning, tracking, zooming and focus for stills, animations or model work.

Saticon Type of camera tube found in some studio and industrial cameras, now being superseded by CCD sensors.

Scanner (1) Mobile production vehicle. (2) Head assembly on a VTR.

Scene dock Storage area for scenery.

Script *Rehearsal script* only contains the actors' lines (dialogue) and basic action (moves). A *camera script* also includes the operational, technical and staging information required for production treatment.

SECAM (Séquence Couleur avec Mémoire) Colour television system used mainly in France and USSR.

Sepmag Film using separate tracks for sound and picture that are synchronised.

Set-up See *Line-up*.

Shadow mask tube Type of display CRT used in colour television receivers and monitors.

Shot An uninterrupted picture from one camera.

Sibilance Sound distortion where some consonants, in particular S sounds, are over-emphasised.

Sidebands The band of frequencies either side of a carrier frequency, resulting from the process of modulation.

Slide scanner Device for producing television pictures from 35 mm slides.

Soft source A light source of large area which produces diffused illumination, and hence soft-edged shadows.

SPG See *Sync pulse generator*.

Split focus Focusing between two objects at different distances from the camera.

Split screen Two or more images displayed separately on different parts of a picture.

Spot (spotlight) Source of light giving well-defined shadows.

Spot effects Live sound effects.

Spring reverb Cheap echo device employing a spring with sound transducers.

Stage weight Heavy weight with hand grip used for restraining scene braces or items of scenery.

Standards conversion Conversion of one picture standard to another, e.g. 625 lines 50 Hz PAL to 525 lines 60 Hz NTSC, and vice versa.

Star filter Camera filter producing symmetrical starlike radiations from highlights, e.g. a light on jewellery.

Still frame Stationary picture from videotape machine or disc.

Storyboard Sequence of drawings to indicate how a story should be shot.

Super (superimpose) Mix two pictures together.

Switcher See *Vision mixer*.

Sync pulse generator (SPG) The heart of the TV studio that produces all the necessary pulses to drive the video equipment.

Synchroniser Digital store for a frame of video that may be read out at a different rate so that pictures can be synchronised with local pictures. May also be used as a basic timebase corrector.

Talkback Communications between production and technical staff.

Tally light 'Camera live' light.

TBC See *Timebase corrector*.

Tearing Ragged effect sometimes seen from chroma key switches when incorrectly set up.

Technical run Rehearsal of a complete programme usually in a rehearsal room for the technicians responsible for lighting, sound and cameras.

Telecine (TK) Machine for replaying film on TV.

Teleprompter Device usually fitted on the front of a camera to enable a performer to read the script whilst looking directly at the camera.

Termination The electrical load value required to match the output impedance of a piece of equipment, or a line.

Test card Studio caption specially designed to enable cameras, monitors and receivers to be lined up.

Throw focus Change focus from foreground to background.

Tie-line Interlinking sound or vision connection routed between technical areas.

Tilt To move a camera through a vertical arc. 'Tilt up' and 'tilt down' refer to the direction the *front* of the camera moves.

Timebase corrector (TBC) Device for eliminating instability in VTR playbacks to make them synchronous at the vision mixer.

Time code Digital signal which uniquely identifies frames, used for synchronising VTRs in editing and for logging purposes when preparing an edit.

TK See *Telecine*.

Tone Audio signal used for sound line-up, usually 1 kHz.

Track (1) Forward or backward movement of a camera. (2) Rails on which a camera can move (used mainly on location on uneven surfaces). (3) Ability of a zoom lens to remain in sharp focus on a subject while the zoom range is altered, i.e. change of shot size.

Track laying Synchronising a number of sound sources on different audio tracks with a picture.

Tracking line Imaginery line on which the camera moves.

Transceiver A combined transmitter and receiver.

Transcoder Device for converting from one colour system to another (but not line or field standards).

Transducer A device for converting one type of energy into another, e.g., loudspeaker converts electrical signals to sound waves.

Trimming tool A tool made of non-magnetic material used for adjusting the position of ferric cores inside coils (i.e. tuning them).

Tungsten Incandescent lamp used for domestic and house lighting having a nominal colour temperature.

Twin track Audio recording using half the width of quarter-inch tape.

TX Transmission.

U-Matic One of the commonest types of videocassette formats of industrial/professional quality (becoming obsolete).

Underscan Reduced width and height of a television picture; used to ensure that all the picture information can be seen and not cut off at the edge of the screen as on domestic receivers, which are overscanned.

Upstage The acting area farthest away from the camera. Hence to walk 'upstage' is to walk away from the camera.

VCR Videocassette recorder.

VDU Visual display unit (usually for text or computer information).

Vectorscope Test equipment used for aligment of colour signals, giving a display of chrominance information in polar form.

VHS Domestic cassette format, now produced as standard play, long play and 'super' for semi-professional use.

Video disc Device for playing back vision and sound on a laser disc resembling an audio compact disc but larger.

Videotape recording Recording of audio and video signals on magnetic tape.

Vidicon Camera tube using a photo-resistive image sensor, now superseded by CCD sensors.

Viewfinder Small monitor on or adjacent to a camera.

Vignette (1) Mask placed in front of a camera to obscure part of a scene. (2) fault occuring with some lenses that reduces light sensitivity at the edges of the picture.

Vision mixer (switcher) (1) Electronic equipment for cutting and mixing picture and for producing a variety of special effects. (2) The person who operates the above equipment.

VT Videotape.

VT clock Videotape leader identifying programme and providing accurate cueing of VT replays.

VTR Videotape recorder generally of the open-reel type (cassette recorders are usually referred to as VCRs)

VU meter (volume unit) Audio meter giving mean audio levels.

Waveform TV signal displayed on an oscilloscope.

Whip pan Rapid pan of a camera.

White Balance Adjustment of camera controls, usually automatic, to ensure correct colour rendition of the camera.

Wild track Audio not synchronised to a picture.

Window The amount of jitter from a VTR that a timebase corrector can handle, usually measured as timing errors in multiples of line (e.g. 2-line window 8-line window).

Windshield A gauze or fabric shield fitted over a microphone to reduce the audible effects of wind, breath, etc.

Wipe Facility on a vision mixer to enable one picture to be replaced with another by a moving edge, or edges.

Wow Variation in speed of a recorder causing audible pitch changes between 1 and 15 per second.

Xenon lamp A discharge type projection lamp having a colour temperature of about 6500 K (the standard for projecting colour film).

XLR Professional audio connector using three pins for balanced or unbalanced audio signals.

Y Symbol used for luminance part of a television signal.

Zero level In audio engineering, a signal equivalent to a sine wave of r.m.s. value 0.775 V (the voltage developed across a resistance of 600 ohms when 1 mW is dissipated in it).

Zoom lens of variable focal length which enables the shot size to be changed over a continuous range, e.g. 14:1.